Makers of Indian Constitution

The daring publisher, Universal Law Publishing Company, among the foremost in the law publishing field and progressive in venturing to bring out rare legal literature of avant garde *character has rightly enriched the* corpus juris *of India*

Justice V R Krishna Iyer
Random Reflections, page 14

Makers of Indian Constitution

Second Edition

Keshav Dayal
Senior Advocate

Universal
Law Publishing Co. Pvt. Ltd.
NEW DELHI - INDIA

First Edition : 2013
Second Edition : 2014

ISBN: 978-93-5035-384-4

Published by

Universal
Law Publishing Co. Pvt. Ltd.
NEW DELHI - INDIA

A-58, G.T. Karnal Road Industrial Area,
(Near Azadpur Metro Station), Delhi-110033
Tel. : 011-47082254, 27458529, 27215334 Fax : 011-27458529
e-mail: unilaw@vsnl.com

- Showroom : C-27, Connaught Place, New Delhi-110001
  e-mail: sales@unilawbooks.com
- Editorial : edit@unilawbooks.com
- Website : **www.unilawbooks.com**

Join us on Facebook
www.facebook.com/unilawbooks

Recommended citation: Keshav Dayal, *Makers of Indian Constitution* 2nd Edn. (New Delhi: Universal Law Publishing Co. Pvt. Ltd., 2014).

Computer Typeset at Aesthetic and *Printed* at Deepak Printers, Delhi.

Preface to the Second Edition

The release of the first edition has been a great satisfaction to me. It was well received and commented upon by the lawyers and the Judges. The book was released in a glittering function on 1st March, 2013. The book was released by Hon'ble Mr. Justice P. Sathasivam, the Chief Justice then Judge, Supreme Court of India. Mr. Soli J. Sorabjee, former Attorney General of India & Senior Advocate presided over the function and Mr. Justice Madan B. Lokur, Judge, Supreme Court was the Chief Guest. The Chief Justice's conversation on this occasion was a memorable one and it also traced the history of the amendments made to the Indian Constitution since its inception. Valuable suggestions made by the learned Judges that the next book should be on the developments on law *viz* all the amendments made in the Constitution of India up till now. Mr. Soli J. Sobarjee also spoke and suggested of incorporating the various speeches made in the Lok Sabha in framing of the Indian Constitution.

The book was presented to the Hon'ble Lt. Governor of Delhi at a very well organized meeting. The book was also presented to the various Vice-Chancellors, including the Vice Chancellors of the Jawaharlal Nehru University and the Indira Gandhi National Open University. All these developments have motivated me in bringing out the revised edition only after a few months of the release of my book "Makers of the Indian Constitution".

I also thought it necessary that the readers of the book should be familiar with the preamble and the basic

Fundamental Rights enunciated in the Constitution of India and now form the part of the revised edition.

My thanks are also largely due to Mr. Anil Kumar Bakshi, Advocate and Mr K.M. Sharma, Advocate for rendering valuable help in bringing out the revised edition. My thanks are also due to Dr. Manish Arora and his dedicated team of Universal Law Publishing Co., New Delhi, in bringing out the revised edition.

September, 2013

KESHAV DAYAL
SENIOR ADVOCATE AND AUTHOR

Preface to the First Edition

India became independent on 15 August, 1947. Indian Constitution was framed in 1949 and adopted on 26 January, 1950. The makers of the Indian Constitution have played a very significant role in Indian History. Many of us, specially the younger generation are however, unaware of the efforts that have gone into making of the present day Constitution. It is absolutely necessary to apprise the incoming and new generation, including the Law Teachers, Members of the Bar and Judiciary about the Historical role played by the Constitution-makers in making of the Indian Constitution of the Indian Republic. The various chapters about the making of the Constitution will throw new insight into the minds of the framers of the Constitution, who had a world-wide vision for the entire country consisting of different cultures and religions.

The book includes the short biographies of Dr. Rajendra Prasad, Pt. Jawaharlal Nehru, Sardar Vallabhbhai Patel, Dr. B.R. Ambedkar, (who were also famous freedom fighters). The book also includes the short biographies of Shri B.N. Rau, Constitutional Advisor, Shri S.N. Mukherjee, Shri H.V.R. Iyenger, Smt. Sarojini Naidu and many others who helped in drafting the Constitution of India, which was finalized on 26th November, 1949, (which is) celebrated as "Law Day" by the Members of the Bar and the Bench.

The present book is relevant and crucial for the present day and future generation of Law students, the Indian Lawyers and the Judiciary. The role played by the prominent leaders including lawyers has become important and is essential for the comprehensive study of the present day Constitution. The study of the biographies of the Constitution-makers is also needed to apprise the present day generation, which is not aware of the historic steps taken in making of the Constitution of India. The study of the biographies of these Constitution-makers will be a source of information and inspiration for the present day generation as well as for the Law Students, Members of the Bar and the Judiciary.

KESHAV DAYAL
Senior Advocate

Gratitude

The role played by the Indian Constitution-makers has been unique and a land mark in the Indian History. However, the present day generation is unaware of the efforts that have gone into making of the present day Constitution, which is a model Constitution not only for the country or the Asian Continent but for the entire world. The Constitution-makers have played a historical role in giving to this country a Constitution which is most suitable to the Indian conditions, but which has also drawn considerable inspiration from other world countries including USA, Ireland and the Commonwealth Countries.

The inspiration of writing this book has come from the good response to my earlier books "Reflections of a lawyer" and "Famous Lawyers of Freedom Struggle and Trial of Freedom Fighters". The Book has won accolades not only from the lawyers and the judges but also from the Cabinet Ministers, Politicians, Governors and most other eminent persons. In fact the present book is a sequel to the book "Famous Lawyers of Freedom Struggle and Trial of Freedom Fighters".

Various Chapters about the making of the Constitution throw new lights into the minds of the framers of the Constitution who had world-wide vision for the entire country consisting of different cultures and religions. The book also includes the biographies of the freedom fighters who were also in the forefront in making of the present day Constitution and which includes Dr. Rajendra Prasad, the First President of India; Pandit Jawaharlal Nehru, the First Prime Minister of India; Sardar Vallabhbhai Patel, the First Home Minister of India and last but not the least, Dr. B.R. Ambedkar, who is known as the father of the Present day Constitution, the First Law Minister of India.

The Book also includes the biographies of Shri B.N. Rau, the Constitutional Advisor, Sh. K.M. Munshi, Sh. A.S. Ayyangar, Smt. Sarojini Naidu, and many others who helped in drafting the Indian Constitution, which was finalized on 26th November, 1949 and this day is celebrated as "Law Day" by the members of the Bar and the Benches.

My thanks are due to various individuals who have helped me in many ways in compilation of this book. I am thankful to Sh. K.M. Sharma, Advocate who helped me in reading and making suggestions in respect of various chapters. I am also thankful to Sh. Sanjay Kumar Singh, Advocate who has been working in my chamber for a number of years. I am also thankful to Shri Anil Bakshi, Advocate-on-Record, Supreme Court who has gone through the manuscript and made valuable suggestions. I am thankful to Shri Manish Arora who has also helped me in completion of this book. I am also thankful to the publisher, Universal Law Publishing Co. Pvt. Ltd., who have always been helpful in publishing my earlier books *viz.* "Reflections of a Lawyer" and "Famous Lawyers of Freedom Struggle and Trials of Freedom Fighters."

I have to place on record my father's life as an ideal lawyer and the image which he carried in the legal profession which has always been a source of unending inspiration for me in all my ventures, including writing the present book.

KESHAV DAYAL
Senior Advocate

RAJ BHAVAN
BANGALORE

2012

Message

I am happy to learn that Shri Keshav Dayal, Senior Advocate has authored the book "Framing of the Indian Constitution and Biographies of Constitution-Makers".

The freedom struggle led by Mahatma Gandhi was a glorious period in Indian history. After attaining Independence, the Constituent Assembly enacted the Constitution of India, which promises Social, Economic and Political Justice to the people of India. The power of Judicial Review vested in Superior Courts is an outstanding feature of our Constitution. India is a vibrant democracy today and people of India enjoy life and liberty.

I have the privilege of knowing Shri Keshav Dayal, Senior Advocate as a very outstanding Member of the Bar and Chief Legal Adviser of Delhi Development Authority. His father late Shri Bishamber Dayal was Senior Standing Counsel for Government in Delhi High Court for decades. Legal fraternity all over the world and particularly in India are admired for their role in freedom struggle and upholding Rule of Law.

Shri Dayal's book will throw light on the great lives of our founding fathers and will indeed inspire generations to come.

I send my good wishes for health and happiness of Shri Keshav Dayal, Senior Advocate.

H.R. BHARDWAJ
Governor of Karnataka

सत्यमेव जयते

Murlidhar C. Bhandare

GOVERNOR, ODISHA

2012

Message

I am glad to know that a book titled "Framing of the Indian Constitution and Biographies of the Constitution-Makers" has been brought out. It is heartening that the book has been greatly appreciated by the Bar, Bench and others.

Beginning from Mahatma Gandhi, Pandit Jawaharlal Nehru and Rajendra Prassad, many other brilliant lawyers were part of Indian freedom movement. Many were the guiding spirit behind the 'Satyagraha' and non-violent agitation in their respective areas. Many others fought court battles for freedom fighters without charging any fee.

The book is a storehouse of rare and important information. Students, academicians and researchers will immensely benefit from the book. Members of the younger generation will find the book interesting as well as informative. Also, the reader will have an insight into the making of the Constitution.

I appreciate the author's commitment and dedication and hope, he will come up with more such works.

I send my best wishes to the author and wish the book great success.

MURLIDHAR C. BHANDARE

सलमान खुर्शीद, सांसद
SALMAN KHURSHID, M.P.

सत्यमेव जयते

मंत्री
विधि एवं न्याय
भारत सरकार
MINISTER OF LAW & JUSTICE
GOVERNMENT OF INDIA

2012

Message

I am delighted that Shri Keshav Dayal, Senior Advocate has written the book, *"Framing of the Indian Constitution and Biographies of the Constitution-Makers"*.

As a member of the Bar, I have had the privilege to know Shri Keshav Dayal over the years. He is a distinguished Senior Advocate of long standing and comes from a family of successful lawyers. His earlier books *"Reflections of a Lawyer"* and *"Famous Lawyers of Freedom Struggle & Trials of Freedom Fighters"* were very well received and widely appreciated by the readers. This book is about the making of the Indian Constitution with useful biographies of eminent personalities who were dramatis personae in the framing of the Constitution.

It is important for all citizens to understand the Constitution and the concepts that are its intellectual building blocks. I expect the book to be widely welcomed by scholars, teachers, lawyers, judges and all enlightened citizens interested in understanding the Constitution of India.

My compliments to the author for his endeavours and best wishes for successful publication.

SALMAN KHURSHID

402, 'A' Wing, Shastri Bhawan, New Delhi-110001, Tel.: 011-23384567/23386615, Fax: 011-23384241

JUSTICE A.K. SIKRI HIGH COURT OF DELHI
ACTING CHIEF JUSTICE SHER SHAH ROAD, NEW DELHI-110003

Ph.: 23387949, 23382951, Fax: 23782731

Message

Shri Keshav Dayal, Senior Advocate has authored the book "Framing of the Indian Constitution and Biographies of the Constitution-Makers". The title of the book itself suggests the prominent role of the eminent and distinguished Constitution makers had played in framing of the Constitution. Shri Keshav Dayal, Senior Advocate has asked me to write a message for this unique book. It is my pleasant task to write a few words for it.

Shri Keshav Dayal is a Senior Advocate of a long standing. He has been the Chief Legal Adviser for Delhi Development Authority. He has an academic bent of mind and keen interest in teaching and writing books. I have known his father, Shri Bishamber Dayal, who was Crown Pleader and Standing Central Government Counsel for a long time. His father has been a great source of inspiration for him.

We need to harness the talent depicted in the biographies of the famous framers of the Indian Constitution who had created Indian Constitution for our present and future generations. This will be a real tribute to all those who had taken part in the framing of the Indian Constitution.

I congratulate Shri Keshav Dayal, Senior Advocate for bringing out the present work. I am sure this book will be of great interest to everyone. In my view, this book would inspire the members of the Bar and the Bench, the law teachers, the students and the citizens of this country.

A.K. SIKRI
Acting Chief Justice

Res: 8, Rajaji Marg, New Delhi - 110 001. Ph.: 23016022, 23016044, E-mail: aksikrij@gmail.com

सत्यमेव जयते

महा - सॉलिसिटर
भारत
SOLICITOR GENERAL OF INDIA

Message

I am happy that Keshav Dayal has written a book on the "Framing of the Indian Constitution and Biographies of the Constitution-Makers". A book of this nature would definitely be found useful by any student of the Constitutional Law of India. I wish him all the best!

ROHINTON F. NARIMAN

Y. K. Sabharwal

Former Chief Justice of India

B-9 Maharani Bagh,
New Delhi-110065
Tel : +911140187362
Fax : +911140817356
Email : yksbharwal@gmail.com

Message

I am extremely delighted to know that Shri Keshav Dayal, Senior Advocate has written - yet another book, namely, 'Framing of the Indian Constitution and Biographies of the Constitution-Makers', which is likely to be released soon.

I have had the pleasure of knowing family of Shri Keshav Dayal who has been a Senior Advocate practicing in Delhi High Court for many decades. Late Shri Bishamber Dayal, father of Shri Keshav Dayal has always been a source of inspiration to Lawyers, particularly young Lawyers. Shri Bishamber Dayal, a renowned Public Prosecutor of his time was highly respected by each and everyone in the legal fraternity including Judges. When I entered legal profession in 1964, I witnessed the amount of respect and regard enjoyed by Shri Bishamber Dayal.

His Book 'Framing of the Indian Constitution and Biographies of the Constitution-Makers' is divided into three parts. Part I, which has two chapters, contains notable quotes and important dates and events. Part III sets out biographies of framers of the Indian Constitution. Part II, the main part of the book has XIV Chapters — Chapter I starting with 'First attempt of making of the Constitution' and last Chapter XIV ending with speech of Dr. Rajendra Prasad, November 25, 1949 and Final adoption of the Constitution. Like earlier publications, this book too, I am confident, will be quite useful to the members of the Bar, Bench and the Law Students.

My best wishes to Shri Keshav Dayal, Senior Advocate.

Y.K. SABHARWAL

BASANT KUMAR JAGGI
NAVIN KUMAR JAGGI
Enrolment No. D/112/1972
TANVI BAKSHI JAGGI
Enrolment No. D/767/2006

JAGGI JAGGI & JAGGI
ATTORNEYS AT LAW
SUPREME COURT OF INDIA

March 4, 2013

Mr. Keshav Dayal
Senior Advocate
209, Lawyers' Chambers
Delhi High Court
New Delhi-110003

Respected Mr. Keshav Dayal,

It was a pleasure to attend the Book Release Ceremony on March 1, 2013 and hear the inspirational words of the elite guests.

Your indefatigable endeavors have ultimately fructified in a remarkable composition, "Framing of the Indian Constitution and Biographies of the Constitution Makers". What is astounding is, that even the Literary and Legal Giants, were not aware of the contribution of sundry other Luminaries in their own field.

Verily, your contribution in this regard is unparalleled and has immortalized you.

I was impressed when Mr. Soli J. Sorabjee, employed the epithet, "cultivated", for you.

312, lawyers' chambers, delhi high court, new delhi-110 003 Tel.: 23782499, 23389410, 23386548
Fax: +91-11-23382516
8, Birbal Road, Ground Floor, Jangpura Extn., New Delhi-110014 PH.: +91-11-24321090
D-996, New Friends colony New Delhi-110 025 Ph.: +91-11-26918110
E-mail: nkja@rediffmail.com tanvibakshijaggi@gmail.com

It was after ages that I came across the word "cultivated", which most appropriately describes a suave, refined, cultured, sophisticated and aristocratic personality.

Mr. Keshav Dayal Sir, you truly deserve this addressal.

Mr. Keshav Dayal Sir, I would like to share with you my experience at the London High Court, in one of my many sojourns thereat.

His Lordship, the then Master of Rolls, Lord Denning, had used this word at a Banquet in honour of the elevation of His Lordship, Sir Mota Singh, the first Indian Judge to be elevated to the highest pedestal of justice.

We were at the Banquet, when we moved in to the Library for a nightcap and cognac. That's when His Lordship informed me that he had noted, how I held my knife and fork at the Banquet Table.

His words still ring in my ears with the loudest decibels - "my peremptory glance convinced me that you are a cultivated gentleman".

Mr. Keshav Dayal Sir, I thank you once again for inviting me for the Book Launch.

May I also take this opportunity of requesting you and Mrs. Dayal, alongwith the family, to join us at 4 pm at Hotel The Ashok', Chanakya Puri, New Delhi on Saturday, 30th March 2013.

Personal regards,

Navin Kumar Jaggi

Navin Kumar Jaggi Advocate

CONTENTS

Preface to the Seond Edition v
Preface to the First Edition vii
Gratitude ix
Message by H.R. Bhardwaj xi
Message by Murlidhar C. Bhandare xii
Message by Salman Khurshid xiii
Message by A.K. Sikri xiv
Message by Rohinton F. Nariman xv
Message by Y.K. Sabharwal xvi
Message by Navin Kumar Jaggi xviii

PART I

CHAPTER I

NOTABLE QUOTES 1

CHAPTER II

IMPORTANT DATES AND EVENTS 6

PART II

CHAPTER I

FIRST ATTEMPT OF MAKING OF THE CONSTITUTION 9

Congress Resolution on Swaraj Constitution December, 1927 9
The Nehru Report, August 1928 10
Swaraj Party Resolution on the White Paper and the Communal Awards, May 1934 13
Congress Resolution on the Joint Parliamentary Committee Report, December 1934 14

CHAPTER II

QUIT INDIA MOVEMENT 15

CHAPTER III

WAVELL PLAN OF 1945 AND CABINET MISSION OF 1946 19

The Wavell Plan of 1945 20
The Simla Conference, July 1945 20

Negotiations – 1944-45 21

Cabinet Mission, 1946 21

CHAPTER IV

ELECTION OF THE MEMBERS OF THE CONSTITUENT ASSEMBLY AND FORMATION OF VARIOUS COMMITTEES 24

CHAPTER V

FORMATION OF VARIOUS COMMITTEES 29

Appointment of Experts' Sub-Committees 29

CHAPTER VI

WORKING OF CONSTITUENT ASSEMBLY 35

Committees under the Constituent Assembly 36

Members of the Indian Constituent Assembly 36

Indian National Congress 36

Muslim League 39

Others 40

List of Members (by province/State) 40

CHAPTER VII

GOODWILL MESSAGES FROM ABROAD ON THE OPENING DAY OF THE CONSTITUENT ASSEMBLY AND THE INAUGURAL ADDRESS BY SACHCHIDANANDA SINHA, PROVISIONAL CHAIRMAN 45

CHAPTER VIII

THE OBJECTIVES' RESOLUTION (DECEMBER 1946 – JANUARY 1947) – PANDIT NEHRU'S SPEECH AND THE SPEECH OF DR. S. RADHAKRISHNAN 51

Nehru's Speech on the Resolution 52

Radhakrishnan's Speech 55

CHAPTER IX

THE QUESTIONNAIRE ISSUED BY THE CONSTITUTIONAL ADVISER – MARCH 17, 1947 57

Questionnaire 57

A: Head of the Indian Union 57

Questionnaire 60
B: Executive 60
Questionnaire 64
C: Legislature 64
Questionnaire 66
D: Judiciary 66
Questionnaire 67
E: Amendment to Constitutions 67

CHAPTER X

AMBEDKAR'S SPEECH MOVING THE DRAFT CONSTITUTION IN THE CONSTITUENT ASSEMBLY – NOVEMBER 4, 1948 69

CHAPTER XI

DRAFT CONSTITUTION AS REVISED BY THE DRAFTING COMMITTEE, NOVEMBER 3rd, 1949 75

CHAPTER XII

CONSTITUENT ASSEMBLY RULES OF PROCEDURE AND STANDING ORDERS AS AMENDED UPTO OCTOBER 15, 1949 79

The Finance and Staff Committee—December 23, 1946 79
The Credentials Committee—December 23, 1946 80
The House Committee—December 23, 1946 80
Sub-committee 81
The Steering Committee—January 21, 1947 81
Order of Business Committee—April-July, 1947 82
Adoption of the National Flag 82

CHAPTER XIII

FUNDAMENTAL RIGHTS 84

Sub-Committee on Minorities 85
Right to Equality (Draft Articles 14–18) 86
Prohibition of the Discrimination (Draft Article 15) 87
Equality of Employment Opportunity (Draft Article 16) 88
Abolition of Untouchability (Draft Article 17) 88
Abolition of Titles (Draft Article 18) 89
Right to Freedom (Draft Articles 19–22) 89
Protection in respect of conviction for offences (Article 20) 90

Protection of Life and Personal Liberty (Article 21) 91
Protection against Arrest and Detention (Article 22) 91
Right against Fxploitation (Articles 23–24) 91
Right to Freedom of Religion (Draft Articles 25–28) 92
Cultural and Educational Rights (Articles 29-30) 94
Right to Property (Article 31) 95
Right to Constitutional Remedies (Article 32-35) 96
Final Shape of Articles on Fundamental Rights 98
Annexure 1—Part III—Fundamental Rights 99

CHAPTER XIV

ADOPTION OF THE CONSTITUTION – NOVEMBER 26, 1949 100

Dr. B.R. Ambedkar's Speech—November 25, 1949 100

CHAPTER XV

SPEECH OF DR. RAJENDRA PRASAD – NOVEMBER 26, 1949 AND FINAL ADOPTION OF THE CONSTITUTION 108

PART III

BIOGRAPHIES OF FAMOUS FRAMERS OF THE INDIAN CONSTITUTION 115

Dr. Rajendra Prasad 117
Pandit Jawaharlal Nehru 121
Dr. Babasaheb Ambedkar 129
Sachchidananda Sinha (1871-1950) 137
Diwan Bahadur Alladi Krishnaswamy Iyer 141
Benegal Narsing Rau 143
K.M. Munshi 147
T.T. Krishnamachari 151
Hansa Mehta 155
N. Gopalaswami Ayyangar 157
Rajkumari Amrit Kaur 159
Sarojini Naidu 163
Bhogaraju Pattabhi Sitaramayya 167
Sardar Vallabhbhai Patel 169
Asaf Ali 181
Subject Index 185

PART I

Chapter I

Notable Quotes

(1) "I wish your labour success, and invoke Divine blessings that your proceedings may be marked not only by good sense, public spirit, and genuine patriotism, but also by wisdom, tolerance, justice, and fairness to all; and above all with a vision which may restore India to her pristing glory, and give her a place of honour and equality amongst the great nations of the world. Let us not forget to justify the pride of the great Indian poet, Iqbal, and his faith in the immortality of the destiny of our great, historic, and ancient country, when he summed up in these beautiful lines:

Yunan-o-Misr-o-Rome sab mit gaye jahan se,
Baqi abhi talak hai nam-o-nishan hamare,
Kuchh bat hai ke hasti mit-ti-nahin hamari,
Sadion raha hai dushman daur-e-zaman hamara."

(Concluding part of the speech of Shri Sachchidanand Sinha, Provisional Chairman on December 9, 1946, on the opening day of the Constituent Assembly)

(2) "Nevertheless, the time comes when we have to rise above party and think of the Nation, think sometimes of even the world at large of which our Nation is a great part. And when I think of the work of this Constituent Assembly, it seems to me, the time has come when we should, so far as we are capable of it, rise above our ordinary selves and party disputes and think of the great

problem before us in the widest and most tolerant and most effective manner so that, whatever we may produce, should be worthy of India as a whole and should be such that the world should recognize that we have functioned, as we should have functioned, in this high adventure."

(3) "As I stand here, Sir, I feel the weight of all manner of things crowding around me. We are at the end of an era, and possible very soon we shall embark upon a new age, and my mind goes back to the great past of India, to the 5,000 years of India's history, form, from the very dawn of that history which might be considered almost the dawn of human history, till today."

(4) "In this Constituent Assembly we are functioning on a world stage and the eyes of the world are upon us and the eyes of our entire past are upon us. Our past is witness to what we are doing here and though the future is still unborn, the future too somehow looks at us, I think, and so, I would beg of this House to consider this Resolution in this mighty prospect of our past, of the turmoil of the present and of the great and unborn future that is going to take place soon."

(Pandit Nehru's speech on the objective Resolution December-1946 – January-1947)

(5) ".....we are actors today in a great historical drama. We are involved in it and therefore we are unable to perceive the large contours of it. This declaration, which we make today, is of the nature of a pledge to our own people and pact with the civilized world".

(Radhakrishnan's speech on commending the resolution moved by Pandit Jawaharlal Nehru)

(6) "On 26th January, 1950, India will be an independent country (cheers). What would happen to her independence? Will she maintain her independence or will she lose it again? This is the first thought that comes to my mind. It is not that India was never an

independent country. The point is that she once lost the independence she had. Will she lose it a second time? Will history repeat itself? It is this thought which fills me with anxiety. This eventuality we must all resolutely guard against. We must be determined to defend our independence with the last drop of our blood (cheers)."

(B.R. Ambedkar's speech on November 25, 1949)

(7) "We must make our political democracy a social democracy as well. Political democracy cannot last unless, there lies at the base of it social democracy. What does social democracy mean? It means a way of life which recognizes liberty, equality and fraternity as the principles of life. These principles of liberty, equality and fraternity are not to be treated as separate items in a trinity. They form a union of trinity in the sense that to divorce one from the other is to defeat the very purpose of democracy."

(8) "Constitution is perfect and the Drafting Committee itself is suggesting certain amendments to improve the Draft Constitution. But the debates in the Provincial Assemblies give me courage to say that the Constitution as settled by the Drafting Committee is good enough to make in this country a start with. I feel that it is workable, it is flexible and it is strong enough to hold the country together both in peace-time and in war-time. Indeed, if I may say so, if things go wrong under the new Constitution, the reason will not be that we had a bad Constitution. What we will have to say is, that Man was vile, Sir, I move."

(9) "They are prepared to have Government for the people and are indifferent whether it is Government of the people and by the people. If we wish to preserve the Constitution in which we have sought to enshrine the principle of Government of the people, for the people and by the people, let us resolve not to be tardy in the recognition of the evils that lie across our path and which

induce people to prefer Government for the people, of Government by the people, nor to be weak in our initiative to remove them. That is the only way to serve the country. I know of no better."

(Dr. B.R. Ambedkar's speech dated November 26, 1949)

(10) "The use of English during the period of transition was considered inevitable for practical reasons and no one need be despondent over this decision, which has been dictated purely by practical considerations. It is duty of the country as a whole now and especially of those whose language is Hindi to shape and develop it as to make it the language in which the composite culture of India can find its expression adequately and nobly."

(Speech of Dr. Rajendra Prasad on November 26, 1949 on final adoption of the Constitution)

(11) "In a world torn with conflicts, in world which even after the devastation of two world wars is still depending on armaments to establish peace and goodwill, we are destined to lay a great part, if we prove true to the teachings of the Father of the Nation and give effect to this Directive Principles of our Constitution."

(12) "I would have linked to have some qualifications laid down for members of the Legislatures. It is anomalous that we should insist upon high qualifications for those who administer or help in administering the law but none for those who make it except that they are elected. A law giver requires intellectual equipment but even more than that capacity to take a balanced view of things, to act independently and above all to be true to those fundamental things of life in one world, to have character."

(13) "Whatever the Constitution may or may not provide, the welfare of the country will depend upon the way in which the country is administered. That will depend upon the men who administer it. After all a

Constitution like a machine is a lifeless thing. It acquires life because of the men who control it and operate it, and India needs today nothing more than a set of honest men who will have the interest of the country before them. It requires men of strong character, men of vision, men who will not sacrifice the interests of the country at large for the sake of smaller groups and areas and who will rise over the prejudices which are born of these differences."

(Concluding Speech of Dr. Rajendra Prasad – November 26, 1949 at the Final Adoption of the Constitution)

Chapter II
Important Dates and Events

17th May, 1927	Motilal Nehru moved a resolution for framing of a Constitution for India to be called "Swaraj Constitution" at Bombay Session of the Congress.
May, 1928	The Conference, appointed a small committee with Motilal Nehru as Chairman to determine the Principles of the Constitution of India.
10th Aug., 1928	The Committee submitted report known as "Nehru Report".
December, 1934	All India Congress Working Committee reiterated its view to draw up the Constitution by a Constituent Assembly.
14th July, 1942	Quit India Resolution adopted by Congress Working Committee.
8th August, 1942	Quit India Movement commenced for freedom of India.
14th June, 1945	British Government issued white paper on India.
29th June, 1946	Indian National Congress and The Muslim League decided to join the Contituent Assembly.

1946	Election held for the Constituent Assembly.
9th December, 1946	First meeting of the Constituent Assembly held in the Central Hall of the Parliament House and Dr. Sachchidanand Sinha was elected as the temporary President of the Constituent Assembly.
11th December, 1946	Dr. Rajindra Prasad as The President and H.C. Mukherjee as the Vice-President were elected in the Constituent Assembly. Shri B.N. Rau was appointed as Constitutional Advisor to the Assembly.
13th December, 1946	The objective resolution moved by Pandit Nehru to declare the basic objective and guiding principle to be kept in view in the process of the Constitution making.
22nd January, 1947	The objective resolution was adopted unanimously by the Constituent Assembly.
17th March, 1947	Questionnaire issued by the Constitutional Advisor, Shri B.N. Rau to the members of the Union Constitutional Committee and the Provincial Constitutional Committees.
22nd July, 1947	National Flag was adopted by the Constituent Assembly.
15th August, 1947	India gained Independence with an impressive flag-hosting

	ceremony at the Red Fort by Pandit Jawaharlal Nehru, the First Prime Minister of India.
21st November, 1947	Muslim League disassociated itself from the Constituent Assembly.
4th November, 1948	Draft Constitution settled by Drafting Committee, introduced in the Constituent Assembly by Chairman of the Drafting Committee, Dr. B.R. Ambedkar.
May, 1949	India became member of Commonwealth.
17th October, 1949	Clause-by-Clause consideration of the Draft Constitution concluded.
3rd November, 1949	Draft Constitution submitted to the President of the Contituent Assembly.
26th November, 1949	Constitution was adopted by the Constituent Assembly on a motion by Dr. B.R. Ambedkar "that the Constitution as settled by the Assembly be passed" this sacred day is celebrated as the "Law Day" by the entire nation.
24th January, 1950	National Anthem adopted.
26th January, 1950	India became Republic and the day is celebrated as "Republic Day" by the entire nation.

PART II

Chapter I

First Attempt of Making of the Constitution*

Congress Resolution on Swaraj Constitution December, 1927

On May 17, 1927, at the Bombay session of the Congress, Motilal Nehru moved a resolution calling upon the Working Committee to frame a Constitution for India in consultation with the elected members of the Central and Provincial legislatures and leaders of political parties and place it before as special meeting of the A.I.C.C. At Hamid Khan's suggestions the word "Constitution" in the original resolution was amended to read "Swaraj Constitution", another amendment moved by Kausulji, to include a Declaration of Rights in the proposed Constitution was accepted by the mover. As so amended, the resolution was adopted by an overwhelming majority. This directive to the Working Committee was, with certain amplifications, reiterated in another resolution adopted at the Madras Congress on December 28, 1927. The need for framing a Constitution for India was also emphasized by M.A. Ansari in his Presidential Speech at the Congress.

In his Presidential Speech Mr. M.A. Ansari expressed his views as under:—

> To "frame (a), Constitution for a people consisting of 320 million souls, professing different religions and speaking different languages, will be

* The Framing of India's Constitution – Select Documents by B. Shiva Rao (Vol. I), pp. 55 to 78 (Universal Law Publishing Co.).

> the most unique and gigantic experiment in democracy ever attempted. The task of the framers will be further complicated by the presence of Indian States exercising sovereign rights in their territories. Whatever be the final form of the constitution, one thing may be said with some degree of certainty, that it will have to be on federal lines providing for a United States of India with existing Indian states as autonomous units of the Federation taking their proper share in the defence of the country, in the regulation of the nation's foreign affairs and other joint and common interests."

The Nehru Report, August 1928

In compliance with the directions contained in the Madras Congress Resolution, 1927, the Working Committee of the Congress convened an All Parties Conference to draft a Swaraj Constitution for India. The first meeting of the Conference, attended, among others, by representatives of the All India Muslim League, the All India Hindu Mahasabha, the Central Khilafat Committee, the All India Conference of Indian Christians, the States' People's Conference, the All India Liberal Federation as well as the Congress was held in February, 1928, at Delhi. The Conference decided that the Constitution to be framed should provide for the establishment of full responsible government. Meeting again in Bombay in May, 1928, the Conference appointed a small committee with Motilal Nehru as the Chairman and seven other members, namely, Ali Imam, Tej Bahadur Sapru, M.S. Aney, Sardar Mangal Singh, Shuaib Qureshi, Subhas Chandra Bose and G.R. Pradhan, commissioning them 'to determine the principles of the Constitution for India'. The report of the Committee (submitted on August 10, 1928), which became famous as 'The Nehru Report', was acclaimed by constitutional historians as "not only an answer to the challenge that Indian nationalism was unconstructive" but the "frankest attempt yet made by Indians to face squarely the difficulties of communalism". In brief, the Constitution embodied in the Report was based on the principle of Dominion Status with full responsible government on the Parliamentary pattern.

The important recommendations made by the Nehru Committee related to the following subjects:—

(1) Constitution Status of India

(2) Operation of the Constitution and Laws

(3) Definition of Citizen

(4) Fundamental Rights

(5) Parliament

(6) The Commonwealth Executive

(7) High Commissioner and Foreign Representatives

(8) Financial Control

(9) The Provincial Legislation

(10) The Provincial Executive, and

(11) The Judiciary.

A reading of the Nehru Report shows in great details in which the Committee had outlined the parameters of the Indian Constitution. The reading of the report also shows a remarkable work undertaken by the Committee. The Swaraj Constitution is similar to a large extent to the Constitution of India as framed by the Constituent Assembly of India. In fact the Swaraj Constitution led the way in framing/making of the present Constitution by the Constituent Assembly of India. Suffice it to know that the said Swaraj Constitution dealt with the subjects of Judiciary and Supreme Court, Defence, Civil Services, Armed Services, and even the provisions relating to the amendment of the Constitution. It will be necessary to at least note the provisions related to the judiciary in the said Constitution.

The said Constitution in relation to the formation and powers of the Supreme Court, is also very illuminating, which are as under:—

"Judiciary: There shall be a Supreme Court which shall exercise such jurisdiction as Parliament shall determine. The Supreme Court shall consist of a Lord President and so many other Justices, as Parliament may fix. The Lord President of the Commonwealth, and all other judges of the Supreme Court of the Commonwealth to be appointed after the establishment of the Commonwealth, shall be appointed by the Governor-General-in-Council, and shall receive such remuneration as Parliament may prescribe, and their remuneration shall not be diminished during their continuance in office. The Lord President of the Commonwealth and other judges of the Supreme Court of the Commonwealth shall not be removed from office except by the Governor-General-in-Council on an address from both Houses of Parliament in the same session praying for such removal on the ground of misbehaviour or incapacity. The Supreme Court shall have original jurisdiction in all matters—(i) referred to the Supreme Court by the Governor-General-in-Council under section 85; (ii) in which the Commonwealth or person suing or being sued on behalf of the Commonwealth, is a party; (iii) affecting consuls or other representatives of other countries; (iv) between provinces; (v) arising under this Constitution or involving its interpretation. The Supreme Court shall have jurisdiction with such exceptions and subject to such regulations as Parliament prescribes, to hear and determine appeals from all judgments, decrees, orders and sentences—(a) of any justice or justices exercising the original jurisdiction of the Supreme

Court; (b) of the High Court of any province, or of any other court of any province from which at the establishment of the Commonwealth an appeal lies to the King-in-Council. The judgment of the Supreme Court in all such cases shall be final and conclusive and shall not be reviewed or be capable of being reviewed by any other court, tribunal or authority whatsoever."

Particularly the clauses relating to the amendment of the Constitution are worthnoting:—

AMENDMENT OF THE CONSTITUTION: "Parliament may, by law, repeal or alter any of the provisions of the Constitution. Provided that the bill embodying such repeal or alteration shall be passed by both Houses of Parliament sitting together and at the third reading shall be agreed to by not less than two-thirds of the total number of the members of both Houses. A Bill so passed at such a joint sitting shall be taken to have been duly passed by both Houses of Parliament."

Swaraj Party Resolution on the White Paper and the Communal Awards, May 1934

In March, 1933, the British Government issued a White Paper outlining their proposals for constitutional reforms in India, which were later examined by a Joint Parliamentary Committee and with some modifications, embodied in the Government of India Act, 1935. The proposals were found unacceptable by nationalist Indian opinion. On May 3, 1934, meeting at Ranchi under the Presidentship of M.A. Ansari, the Swaraj Party Conference passed a resolution rejecting the White Paper proposals and demanding the convening of a Constituent Assembly to frame an acceptable Constitution for India. This was the first time that the demand for a Constitution Assembly for India as such was formally put forward.

Congress Resolution on the Joint Parliamentary Committee Report, December 1934

The Working Committee of the All-India Congress Committee at its meeting held on December 5-7, 1934 at Patna adopted a resolution rejecting the scheme of Indian Constitutional Reforms recommended in the Report of the Joint Parliamentary Committee (1933-34), and reiterating its view that the only satisfactory alternative to the scheme was a Constitution drawn up by a Constituent Assembly.

It was, therefore, abundantly clear that the Working Committee of the All India Congress Committee reiterated its view that the only satisfactory alternative to the scheme was a Constitution drawn up by the Constituent Assembly.

How true it came to be as the present Constitution in fact drawn up by the Constituent Assembly, which was a vision of the Resolution of the Working Committee of the All India Congress Committee as early as in 1936. The present generation and the framers of the present Indian Constitution owe a lot to the efforts made by the Nehru Committee in framing of the Swaraj Constitution.

Chapter II
Quit India Movement

The history of the Constituent Assembly and framing of the Indian Constitution *viz.* formation of "Sovereign, Secular, Democratic Republic of India would not be complete without mentioning the important events leading to the formation of the Constituent Assembly. The first and the foremost event which shaped the destiny of the Nation in formation of the Constituent Assembly is the Quit India Movement. The history starts with the historic resolution adopted by the Congress calling upon the Britishers to Quit India, passed at Bombay on August 8, 1942, when it approved the resolution earlier adopted by its working committee on July 14, 1942, which came to be known as 'Quit India' resolution, which marked the commencement of the historic Quit India Movement of 1942.

The Committee resolves, (therefore), to sanction for the vindication of India's inalienable right to freedom and independence, the starting of a mass struggle on non-violent lines on the widest possible scale, so that the country might utilize all the non-violent strength it has gathered during the last twenty-two years of peaceful struggle. Such a struggle must inevitably be under the leadership of Gandhiji and the committee requests him to take the lead and guide the nation in the steps to be taken.

'Quit India' 'Bharat Chhoro' – The simple but powerful slogan launched the legendary struggle which also became famous by the name of the "August Revolution'. In this struggle, the common people of the country demonstrated an unparalleled heroism and militancy. Moreover, the repression that they faced was the most brutal that had ever been used against the national movement. The circumstances in which the resistance was offered were also the most adverse faced by the national movement until then using the justification of the war effort, the Government had armed itself with draconian measures, and suppressed even basic civil liberties. Virtually any political activity, however peaceful and 'legal', was at this time an illegal and revolutionary activity. The sudden attack by the Government produced an instantaneous reaction among the people. In Bombay, as soon as the news of arrests spread, lakhs of people flocked to Gowalia Tank where a mass meeting had been scheduled and there were clashes with the authorities. There were similar disturbances on 9 August in Ahmedabad and Poona. On the 10th, Delhi and many towns in U.P. and Bihar, including Kanpur, Allahabad, Varanasi and Patna followed suit with hartals, public demonstrations and processions in defiance of the law. The Government responded by gagging the press. The National Herald and Harijan ceased publication for the entire duration of the struggle, others for shorter periods.

The Working Committee of the Congress Meet at Wardha on 14th July, 1942 accepted the idea of struggle, The All India Congress Committee meeting in August, Gandhiji's speech was historic. He made a statement that 'nothing less than freedom was acceptable". He gave famous exhortation as—

> "Here is a mantra, a short one that I give you. You may imprint it on your hearts and let every breath of yours give expression to it. The mantra is: "Do or Die". We shall either free India or die in the attempt; we shall not live to see the perpetuation of our slavery.

Gandhiji's speech contained specific instructions for sections of the people including Government Servants, Soldiers, Princes and even students.

According to official estimates, in the first week after the arrests of the leaders, 250 railway stations were damaged or destroyed, and over 500 post offices and 150 police stations were attacked. The movement of trains in Bihar and Eastern U.P., remained disrupted for many weeks. In Karnataka alone, there were 1600 incidents of cutting of telegraph lines, and twenty-six railway stations and thirty-two post offices were attacked. Unarmed crowds faced police and military firing on 538 occasions and they were also machine-gunned by low-flying aircraft.

By the end of 1942, over 60,000 persons had been arrested. Twenty-six thousand people were convicted and 18,000 detained under the Defence of India Rules. Martial law had not been proclaimed, but the army, though nominally working under the orders of the civilian authorities, often did what it wanted to without any reference to the officers. The repression was as severe as it could have been under martial law.

A significant feature of the Quit India Movement was the emergence of what came to be known as parallel governments in some parts of the country. The first one was proclaimed in Balia in UP in August, 1942; in Midnapore district of Bengal, the Jatiya Sarkar came into existence on 17th December, 1942 and Satara in Maharashtra emerged as the base of the longest-lasting and effective parallel government.

The Quit India Movement marked a new high in terms of popular participation in the National Movement and sympathy with the National cause. As in earlier mass struggles, the youth were in the forefront of the struggle. Students from colleges and even schools were the most visible element, especially in the early days of August (probably the average age of participation in the 1942 struggle was even lower than that in earlier movements) Women, especially college and school girls, played a very important role. Aruna Asaf Ali and Sucheta Kriplani were two major women organizers of the underground.*

The great significance of this historic movement was that it placed the demand for independence on the immediate agenda of the national movement. After 'Quit India', there could be no retreat. Any future the transfer of power. Independence was no longer matter of bargain. And this became amply clear after the War.

---

* Bipan Chandra's "Indian Struggle for Independence".

Chapter III

Wavell Plan of 1945 and Cabinet Mission of 1946

Soon after the War in Europe came to an end, on June 14, 1945, the British Government issued a White Paper on India. The White Paper repeated the Cripps Offer in its entirety. As an interim arrangement, that is, pending the framing of a new Constitution by Indians themselves, it was proposed to reconstitute the Viceroy's Executive Council so as to make it more representative of organized political opinion. The new proposals, which, as Amery, the Secretary of State for India, observed in the House of Commons, 'owed everything to the initiative' of Wavell, the then Viceroy of India, came to be popularly known as the 'Wavell Plan'. On the same day, while explaining the proposals in a broadcast from New Delhi, the Viceroy announced that important leaders of the Indian National Congress, the Muslim League and some other political parties were being invited to a conference of India to discuss the question of forming a new Executive Council. He also disclosed that orders had been given for the immediate release of the members of the Congress Working Committee who were still in detention.

Inter-alia in the Viceroy's broadcast of June, 1945 it was stated as under:—

> "A further step proposed by His Majesty's Government is the appointment of a British High

---

Page 136—The Framing of India's Constitution - Select Documents by B. Shiva Rao (Vol. 1).

Page 140-141—The Framing of India's Constitution - Select Documents by B. Shiva Rao (Vol. 1).

Commissioner in India, as in the Dominions, to represent Great Britain's commercial and other such interests in India.

It was further stated that such a new Executive Council will realize, represent a definite advance on the road to self-government. It will be almost entirely Indian, and the Finance and Home Members will for the first time be, Indians, while an Indian will also be charged with the management of India's Foreign Affairs. Moreover Members will now be selected by the Governor-General after consultation with political leaders; though their appointment will of course be subject to the approval of His Majesty, the King-Emperor."

Further it was stated with the approval of his Majesty's Government, and after consultation with my Council, orders have been given for the immediate release of the members of the Working Committee of Congress who are still in detention as a result of the 1942 disturbances to the new Central Government, if formed, and to the Provincial Governments.

The Wavell Plan of 1945

Then came the 'Wavell Plan' formulated by Lord Wavell the then Viceroy of India under which a representative Government was proposed to be established and vested with large powers, but working under the then existing Constitution. A white paper was published to that effect on June 14, 1945 which was followed by a broadcast by the Viceroy, on behalf of His Majesty.

The Simla Conference, July 1945

The Simla Conference for negotiations between Congress and the Muslim League opened on June 25, 1945, as proposed in Wavell's broadcast of June 14, but was unable to agree upon the strength and composition of the Executive Council. A solution suggested by the

Viceroy was rejected by Jinnah, who was the main spokesman of the Muslim League. In a statement made at the Conference on July 14, the Viceroy announced the failure of the Simla Conference."

Negotiations - 1944-45

The negotiations between 1944-45 also did not result in any agreement, as there was no agreement between Congress and the Muslim League. Gandhiji and Jinaah talks between September 9, 1944 till 27th September also resulted in a failure.

Cabinet Mission, 1946

After the Labour Party had come to power in England, on February 19, it was announced that a Mission of three Cabinet Minsters[1] would be sent out to India to explore the possibility of an immediate settlement of the Indian problem. On March 15, 1946, Mr. Attlee, the Labour Prime Minster declared in the House of Commons: "Is it any wonder that today India claims, as a nation of 400 million people that has twice sent her sons to die for freedom, that she should herself have freedom to decide her own destiny? What form of government is to replace the present regime is for India to decide; but our desire is to help her to set-up forthwith the machinery for making that decision." Thus there was a definite change in attitude of the British Government. It was an unequivocal acceptance of the claim of India to freedom.

The three Ministers arrived in India in March. In April they interviewed many Indian leaders of all parties and groups. A conference was held in Simla with the representatives of the Congress and the Muslim League. As no settlement could be arrived at, the decision of the Mission was announced on May 16, 1946.

1. Lord Pethick-Lawrence, the Secretary of State for India, Sir Stafford Cripps, the President of the Board of the Trade and Mr. A.V. Alexander, the First Lord of Admiralty.

The Congress and the Muslim League having failed to reach an agreement, the Cabinet Mission issued on May 16, 1946, a statement putting forward their own proposals regarding the basic form of the future Constitution and the setting-up of the constitution-making machinery. The Mission rejected the idea of a separate sovereign State of Pakistan.

The Cabinet Mission recommended that the Constitution should take the following basic form:—

(I) There should be a Union of India, embracing both British India and the States, which should deal with the following subjects: Foreign Affairs, Defence, and Communications; and should have the powers necessary to raise the finances required for the above subjects.

(II) The Union should have an Executive and a Legislature constituted from British Indian and States representatives. Any question raising a major communal issue in the Legislature should require for its decision a majority of the representatives present and voting of each of the two major communities as well as a majority of all the members present and voting.

(III) All subjects other than the Union subjects and all residuary powers should vest in the Provinces.

(IV) The States will retain all subjects and powers other than those ceded to the Union.

(V) Provinces should be free to form Groups with executives and legislatures and each Group could determine the Provincial subjects to be taken in common.

(VI) The Constitutions of the Union and of the Groups should contain a provision whereby any Province could, by a majority vote of its

Legislative Assembly, call for a reconsideration of the terms of the Constitution after an initial period of 10 years and at 10 yearly intervals thereafter.

The Indian National Congress found the Cabinet Mission plan unsatisfactory in many respects and the Muslim League also regretted that the Congress initially rejected the demand for Pakistan. The Cabinet Mission gave an explanatory statement in May, 1946.

However, on June 6, 1946, the Council of All India Muslim League passed a resolution which, while critical of the contends of the Cabinet Mission's statement of May 16, 1946, particularly on the issue of Pakistan, and while reiterating that a complete sovereign Pakistan still remained 'the unalterable objective of the Muslims in India' accepted the Mission's plan and announced the League's decision to join the constitution-making body.

Subsequently, by a resolution adopted on June 25, 1946, the Congress Working Committee announced that notwithstanding its dissatisfaction with certain features of the Cabinet Mission's statement of May 16, it had decided that the Congress should join the proposed Constituent Assembly.

The Cabinet Mission left India on June 29, 1946. In a statement issued on June 26, the Mission and the Viceroy welcomed the decisions of the Indian National Congress and the Muslim League to join the Constituent Assembly.

However, subsequently by a resolution adopted on July 27-29, the Council of the All-India Muslim League decided to withdraw its earlier acceptance of the Cabinet Mission's Plan of May 16 and to boycott the Constituent Assembly.

Chapter IV
Election of the Members of the Constituent Assembly and Formation of Various Committees

The Cabinet Mission's Statement of May 16, 1946 had set out in detail procedure regarding elections to the Constituent Assembly. The Cabinet Mission also gave election analysis showing the relative strength of political parties. The important personalities, amongst others elected to the Constituent Assembly consisted of the following:—

(a) Party Leaders

(i) President of the Indian National Congress: Jawaharlal Nehru.

(ii) President of the All-India Muslim League: Mahomed Ali Jinnah.

(iii) President-in-Chief of the Anglo-Indian Association: Frank Reginald Anthony

(iv) President of the All-India Hindu Mahasabha: Syama Prasad Mookerjee

(v) Leader of the All-India Scheduled Castes Federation: B.R. Ambedkar

(vi) President of the All-India Depressed Classes League: Jagjivan Ram

(vi) President of the All-India Women's Conference: Mrs. Hansa Mehta

(b) Premiers of Provinces

(1) T. Prakasam (Madras) – Congress
(2) B.G. Kher (Bombay) – Congress
(3) Harekrushna Mahtab (Orissa) – Congress
(4) Govind Ballabh Pant (U.P.) – Congress
(5) R.S. Shukla (C.P.) – Congress

(c) Ministers of Provinces

(1) Mrs. Vijaya Lakshmi Pandit (U.P.) – Congress
(2) Kailash Nath Katju (U.P.) – Congress
(3) Rafi Ahmed Kidwai (U.P.) – Congress.
(4) Anugraha Narayan Sinha (Bihar) – Congress.
(5) Mehr Chand Khanna (N.W.F.P.) – Congress.

And 5 other Members from Punjab, Sind and Assam.

(d) Ex-Premiers of Provinces

(e) Ex-Ministers or Ex-Members of Governor's Executive Council

(f) Ex-Members of Governor-General's Executive Council

(g) Speakers of Provinces

Purushottamdas Tandon (U.P.) – Congress

(h) Ex-Speakers of Provinces

Sardar Bahadur Khan

(i) Ex-High Court Judges

Bakshi Tek Chand (Punjab)

(j) Ex-Dewans of States

N. Gopalaswami Ayyangar

Women Elected to the Constituent Assembly

There were 15 women in the list including the following:

Mrs. Durga Bai (Madras) – Congress

Rajkumari Amrit Kaur (C.P.) – Congress

Mrs. Sarojini Naidu (Bihar) – Congress.

Vijay Laxmi Pandit (U.P.) – Congress

(k) Province-wise list of members elected to the Constituent Assembly

(1) Madras:

(i) C. Rajagopalachari (Member of the Congress Working Committee, Former Premier of Madras.

(ii) Pattabhi Sitaramayya (Former member of the Congress Working Committee).

(iii) T. Prakasam (Premier of Madras)

(iv) N. Gopalaswami (Member of the Ayyangar Council of State, Former Prime Minister of Kashmir).

(v) Alladi Krishnaswami Ayyar (Former Advocate-General of Madras)

(2) Bombay:

(i) Vallabhbhai Patel (Member, Congress Working Committee, Former Congress President.

(ii) B.G. Kher (Premier of Bombay).

(3) Orissa: Harekrishna Mehtab (Premier of Orissa, Former Member of the Congress Working Committee).

(4) Bihar:

(i) Rajendra Prasad (Member of the Congress Working Committee, Former Congress President.)

(ii) Jagjivan Ram (M.L.A., Provincial).

(5) Delhi:

(i) Asaf Ali (Congress: M.L.A., Central).

(6) Punjab:

(i) Bakshi Tek Chand (Former Judge of Lahore High Court).

(7) North-West Frontier Province:

(i) Abul Kalam Azad (Former President of the Indian National Congress, Member of the Congress Working Committee).

(ii) Abdul Ghaffar Khan (Member of the Congress Working Committee).

(8) Bengal:

(i) Frank Reginald Anthony (President, Anglo-Indian Association).

(9) Assam:

(1) Gopinath Bardoloi (Premier of Assam).

(l) United Provinces:

(1) Jawaharlal Nehru (President of the Indian National Congress).

(2) Purushottamdas Tandon (Speaker of the U.P., Legislative Assembly).

(3) Govind Ballabh Pant (Premier of U.P., Member of the Congress Working Committee).

(4) S. Radhakrishnan (Vice-Chancellor of the Banaras Hindu University).

(5) J.B. Kripalani (Former General-Secretary of the Indian National Congress).

Mr. Jinnah made a statement on 21st November, 1947 that the Muslim League had finally dissociated from the Constituent Assembly.

While the elections to the Constituent Assembly were still in progress, on July 8, 1946, the Congress Working Committee appointed an Experts' Committee for the purpose of preparing material for the Constituent Assembly.

The Experts' Committee consisted of: Jawaharlal Nehru (Chairman), Asaf Ali, K.M. Munshi, N. Gopalaswami Ayyangar, K.T. Shah, D.R. Gadgil, Humayun Kabir and K. Santhanam.

Note: Many of the members of the Constituent Assembly have not been scribed due to lack of knowledge about them.

Chapter V
Formation of Various Committees

Appointment of Experts' Sub-Committees

While the elections to the Constituent Assembly were still in progress, on July 8, 1946, the Congress Working Committee appointed an Experts' Committee for the purpose of preparing material for the Constituent Assembly. The Experts' Committee consisted of: Jawaharlal Nehru (Chairman), Asaf Ali, K.M. Munshi, N. Gopalaswami Ayyangar, K.T. Shah, D.R. Gadgil, Humayun Kabir and K. Santhanam. The Committee had two sittings, the first at New Delhi from July 20 to 22 and the second at Bombay from August 15 to 17. Apart from a number of notes prepared by its members the committee discussed the procedure to be adopted by the Constituent Assembly, the question of the appointment of various committees, and the draft of a resolution on the objectives of the Constitution to be moved during the first session of the Assembly. The basic principles embodied in the resolution were reiterated in a resolution adopted by the Congress Working Committee on November 20, the day the Constituent Assembly was formally summoned.

On December 10, 1946, Acharya Kripalani moved a resolution for the appointment of a committee on the Constituent Assembly Rules of Procedure. It was adopted on the same day with a number of modifications. The most important of the amendments, which were eventually carried by the House, was the one laying down specifically that the Constituent Assembly was competent to frame rules for the Sections and the Committees. The amendment was moved by Suresh Chandra Banerjee and supported by a number of other members, including Syama Prasad Mookherjee, Purushottamdas Tandon, Harnam Singh and K.M. Munshi. The amendment was intended to make it clear that the Assembly was one and indivisible and the Sections were not independent bodies which could provide for procedure inconsistently with the rules of the Assembly. Later, on the same day, the temporary Chairman, Dr. Sachchidananda Sinha, announced that nominations for elections to the Rules Committee were to be filed by 12 noon on the following day. As only 15 nominations were put in, the necessity of an election by ballot was unnecessary and all the candidates proposed, namely: Jag Jivan Ram, Sarat Chandra Bose, P.R. Anthony, Alladi Krishnaswami Ayyar, Bakshi Tek Chand, Rafi Ahmad Kidwai, (Mrs.) G. Durga Bai, Joseph Alban D'Souza, N. Gopalaswami Ayyangar, Purushottamdas Tandon, Gopinath Bardoloi, Dr. B. Pattabhi Sitaramayya, K.M. Munshi, Mehar Chand Khanna and Sardar Harnam Singh stood elected.

The rules *viz.*, the Constituent Assembly rules provided for the business of the Assembly, in all the Assembly, appointments of President, Vice-Presidents and various Committees. The business of the Constituent Assembly was referred to in rule 6(1) of the Business of the Constituent Assembly.

Business of the Assembly:

6. (1) The business of the Assembly means the business conducted—

(i) In the Assembly itself;

(ii) In the Committee of the whole Assembly;

(iii) In the sections;

(iv) In the Advisory Committee referred to in paragraph 20 of the Statement;

(v) In the Steering Committee;

(vi) In the Staff and Finance Committee;

(vii) In the Credentials Committee; and

(viii) In such other committees or sub-committees as may be set up by the Assembly or the Sections or the Advisory Committee or other Committee.

(2) The business of the Assembly shall be conducted in New Delhi unless the Assembly resolves otherwise.

(3) The conduct of the business of the Assembly and the procedure thereof shall be regulated by the rules and standing orders and the resolutions of the Assembly and by the rulings given from time-to-time by the Chairman.

18. (1) The Assembly business was to be transacted in Hindustani (Hindi, or Urdu) or English, provided that the Chairman may permit any member unacquainted with either language to address the Assembly in his mother-tongue.

These Committees were provided in Chapter 7 of the said rules and the rule 38 provided for various committees is quoted below:—

(1) A Steering Committee shall be set up for the duration of the Assembly and shall consist initially of eleven members to be elected by the Assembly in accordance with the principle of proportional representation by means of the single transferable vote.

(2) The Assembly may from time-to-time elect, in such manner as it may deem appropriate, eight additional members, of who four shall be reserved for election from amongst the representatives of the Indian States.

(3) The President shall be an *ex-officio* member of the Steering Committee. The Committee may elect a Vice-Chairman from amongst its

members to preside over the committee in the absence of the President.

(4) The Secretary of the Assembly shall be *ex-officio* Secretary of the Steering Committee.

(5) Casual vacancies in the committee shall be filled as soon as possible after they occur by election by the Assembly in such manner as it may determine.

39. (1) The committee shall—

(a) Arrange the order of business for the day;

(b) Group similar motions and amendments and secure, if possible, assent of the parties concerned to composite motions and amendments;

(c) Act as a general liaison body between the Assembly and its Office, between the Assembly and the Sections, between the Sections *inter se,* between Committees *inter se,* and between the President and any part of the Assembly; and

(d) Deal with any other matter under the rules or referred to it by the Assembly or the President.

(2) President may make standing orders for the conduct of the business of the Steering Committee.

40. (1) A staff and Finance Committee shall be set-up consisting of—

1. The President;
2. The five Vice-Presidents; and
3. Nine other members to be elected in such manner as may be determined by the President.

The functions of the committee shall be—

2. To advise the President regarding the posts to be created in the Office of the Assembly, and the salaries and emoluments to be attached thereto;

3. To recommend to the Assembly the allowances to be paid to the officers and members of the Assembly and its committee;
4. To frame a budget or supplementary budget for submission to the Assembly; and
5. The President may make standing orders for the conduct of the business of the committee.

The finance and staff committee shall invite the Auditor-General to audit the accounts of the Assembly.

41. A Credential Committee shall be set up for the duration of the Assembly for the purpose of dealing with all questions relating to the validity of the title of elected or other members.

42. The Committee shall consist of five members who shall be elected by the Assembly.

(1) The Committee shall have power to co-opt additional members not exceeding two in number.

(2) Casual vacancies in the committee shall be filled as soon as they occur by election or by the Assembly or by co-option, as the case may be.

43. (1) Any other committee may be set up by a motion in the Assembly or a Section according as the business of the committee relates to the Assembly or the Section.

(2) The members of every such committee shall be elected according to the principle of proportional representation by means of the single transferable vote.

(3) The Secretary of the Assembly shall be *ex-officio* Secretary of every such committee, unless the motion by which the committee is set up otherwise provides, and the Secretary of any Section shall be *ex-officio* Secretary of every committee set up by that section, unless the motion by which the committee is set up otherwise provides.

(4) Unless the motion by which a committee is set up otherwise provides, the committee shall appoint one of its members as Chairman who shall regulate the work of the committee

44. The motion by which a committee is to be set up shall state the quorum necessary to constitute a meeting of the committee and the time within which the committee shall present its report.

Page-326: The Framing of India's Constitution – Select Documents by B. Shiva Rao (Vol. 1).

Page-422: The Framing of India's Constitution – Select Documents by B. Shiva Rao (Vol. 1).

Page-426: The Framing of India's Constitution – Select Documents by B. Shiva Rao (Vol. 1).

Page-428: The Framing of India's Constitution – Select Documents by B. Shiva Rao (Vol. 1).

Pages 432-434: The Framing of India's Constitution – Select Documents by B. Shiva Rao (Vol. 1).

Chapter VI
Working of Constituent Assembly

December 9, 1946: The first meeting of Constituent Assembly was held in the constitution hall (now 'Central Hall of Parliament House'). Demanding a separate state, the Muslim League boycotted the meeting. Dr. Sachchidanand Sinha was elected as temporary President of Assembly following the French practice.

December 11, 1946: Elected Dr. Rajendra Prasad and H.C. Mukherjee as the President and Vice-President of the Assembly respectively. Appointed Sir B.N. Rau as Constitutional advisor to the Assembly.

December 13, 1946: 'Objective Resolution' was introduced by Jawaharlal Nehru. Underlying principles of Constitution were laid by Objective Resolution.

January 22, 1947: Unanimously adopted the Objective Resolution.

May 1949: It ratified India's membership of the Commonwealth.

July 22, 1947: Adopted the national flag.

January 24, 1950: Adopted the national anthem, national song. Elected Dr. Rajendra Prasad as the first President of India.

Assembly was chaired by Dr. Rajendra Prasad whenever it met as Constituent body and by G.V. Mavlankar when it met as the legislative body. Constituent Assembly completed the task of drafting Constitution in 2 years, 11 months and 17 days. The total expenditure incurred was Rs. 64 lakh.

Committees under the Constituent Assembly

Committee on the Rules of procedure – *Rajendra Prasad*

Drafting Committee – *B.R. Ambedkar*

Steering Committee – *Rajendra Prasad*

Finance and Staff Committee – *Rajendra Prasad*

Credential Committee – *Alladi Krishnaswamy Iyer*

Languages Committee – *Moturi Satyanarayana*

House Committee – *B. Pattabhi Sitaramayya*

Order of Business Committee – *K.M. Munshi*

Ad hoc Committee on the National Flag – *Rajendra Prasad*

Committee on the Functions of the Constituent Assembly *G.V. Mavalankar*

States' Committee – *Jawaharlal Nehru*

Advisory Committee on Fundamental Rights, Minorities

Tribal and Excluded Areas – *Vallabhbhai Patel*

Minorities Sub-Committee – *Harendra Coomar Mookerjee*

Fundamental Rights Sub-Committee – *J.B. Kripalani*

North-East Frontier Tribal Areas and Assam. Excluded & Partially Excluded Areas Sub-Committee *Gopinath Bardoloi*

Excluded and Partially Excluded Areas (Other than those in Assam) Sub-Committee – *A.V. Thakkar*

Union Powers Committee – *Jawaharlal Nehru*

Union Constitution Committee – *Jawaharlal Nehru*

Members of the Indian Constituent Assembly

Indian National Congress

Pandit Jawaharlal Nehru, 1st Prime Minister

Sardar Vallabhbhai Patel, Deputy Prime Minister-cum-Home Minister

Bhimrao Ramji Ambedkar, Minister for Law, Chairman of Drafting Committee

Maulana Azad, Minister for Education,

Dr. Rajendra Prasad, Chairman of the Assembly

C. Rajagopalachari, Governor-General

Sarat Chandra Bose

Sri Krishna Sinha, Chief Minister, Bihar

Shyam Nandan Prasad Mishra

Anugrah Narayan Sinha, Deputy Chief Minister-cum-Finance Minister, Bihar

Rafi Ahmed Kidwai

Asaf Ali

Sri Sheik Galib Sahib

Syama Prasad Mookerjee, President, Hindu Mahasabha

Moturi Satyanarayana, Freedom Fighter

Rajkumari Amrit Kaur, Minister for Health

Hansa Mehta, President, All India Women's Conference

Prof. N.G. Ranga

Deep Narayan Singh

P. Subbarayan

Kailashnath Katju

N.G. Ayyangar

T.T. Krishnamachari

Rameshwar Prasad Sinha

Durgabai Deshmukh

K.M. Munshi

Krishana Ballabh Sahay

Frank Anthony, Anglo-Indian representative

Sarvepalli Radhakrishnan

Dr. John Mathai

Pratap Singh Kairon
Prof. Shibbanlal Saxena
R.K. Shanmukham Chetty
Alladi Krishnaswamy Iyer
Jagjivan Ram, President, All-India Depressed Classes League
Pandit Govind Ballabh Pant, Premier, United Provinces
Minoo Masani
Renuka Ray
Purushottam Das Tandon
Mahavir Tyagi
Thakur Das Bhargava
Bhagwan Das
Feroze Gandhi
B. Shiva Rao
Jairamdas Daulatram
Pattom A. Thanu Pillai
R. Sankar
P.S. Nataraja Pillai
K.A. Mohamed
P.T. Chacko, Pullolil
Panampilly Govinda Menon
Annie Mascarene
Bhograju Pattabhi Sitaramayya
Kamraj
Ammu Swaminathan
Purnima Banerjee
Vijayalakshmi Pandit
Ramnath Goenka, Editor of the Indian Express
Sarojini Naidu

Jaipal Singh Munda, President, Adibasi Mahasabha

Jagjivan Ram

Dakshayani Velayudan

Revd. Jerome D'Souza

Revd. J.J.M. Nichols-Roy

Gopinath Bordoloi

Dharanidhar Basumatari

Malati Choudhury

Homi Mody

Leela Roy

Biswanath Das, Premier of Orissa

Acharya Kripalani

Sucheta Kripalani

Harendra Coomar Mookerjee

Gopi Krishna Vijayvargiya

Pandit Raghunath Vinayak Dhulekar

D.H. Chandrasekharaiya

Nibaran Chandra Laskar

Ari Bahadur Gururng, Gorkha Community (Darjeeling)

Choudhry Puru

Harsh K. Soni.

Muslim League

Begum Aizaz Rasul, Vice-President (later President) Muslim League (India)

Manuj Bansal

Nawab Mohammad Ismail Khan

Kazi Syed Karimuddin

Chaudhry Khaliquzzaman, President, Muslim League (India)

Naziruddin Ahmad

Z.H. Lari

Mohammad Saadullah, Premier of Assam

Aziz Ahmed Khan

Maulana Daud Ghazhnavi

Tajammul Hussain

Hussain Imam

Mahboob Ali Baig Sahib Bahadur

Pocker Sahib Bahadur

Choudhry Puru

Others

Scheduled Caste Federation

Dr. Ambedkar

Akalis

Sardar Hukam Singh

Communist

Somnath Lahiri

List of Members (by province/State)

Madras O. V. Alagesan, Mrs. Ammu Swaminathan, M. Ananthasayanam Ayyangar, Moturi Satyanarayana, Mrs. Dakshayani Velayudhan, Mrs. G. Durgabai, Kala Venkatarao, N. Gopalaswamy Ayyangar, D. Govinda Das, Revd. Jerome D'Souza, P. Kakkan, T.M. Kaliyannan Gounder, K. Kamaraj, V.C. Kesava Rao, T.T. Krishnamachari, Alladi Krishnaswamy Iyer, L. Krishnaswami Bharathi, P. Kunhiraman, Mosalikanti Thirumala Rao, V.I. Muniswamy Pillay, M.A. Muthiah Chettiyar, V. Nadimuthu Pillai, S. Nagappa, P.L. Narasimha Raju, B. Pattabhi Sitaramayya, C. Perumalswamy Reddy, T. Prakasam, S.H. Prater, Raja Swetachalapati Ramakrishna Renga Rao of Bobbili, R.K. Shanmukham Chetti, T.A. Ramalingam Chettiyyar,

Ramnath Goenka, O.P. Ramaswamy Reddiyar, N.G. Ranga, Neelam Sanjeeva Reddy, Sri Sheik Galib Sahib, K. Santhanam, B. Shiva Rao, Kallur Subba Rao, U. Srinivasa Mallayya, P. Subbarayan, C. Subramaniam, V Subramaniam, M.C. Veerabahu, P.M. Velayudapani, A.K. Menon, T.J.M. Wilson, Mohamed Ismail Sahib, K.T.M. Ahmed Ibrahim, Mahboob Ali Baig Sahib Bahadur, B. Pocker Sahib Bahadur

Bombay: Balchandra Maheshwar Gupte, Mrs. Hansa Mehta, Hari Vinayak Pataskar, B.R. Ambedkar, Joseph Alban D'Souza, Kanayalal Nanabhai Desai, Keshavrao Marutirao Jedhe, Khandubhai Kasanji Desai, Bal Gangadhar Kher, M.R. Masani, K.M. Munshi, Narahar Vishnu Gadgil, S. Nijalingappa, S.K. Patil, Ramchandra Manohar Nalavade, R.R. Diwakar, Shankarrao Deo, G.V. Mavalankar, Vallabhbhai Patel, Abdul Kadar Mohammad Shaikh, A.A. Khan

West Bengal: Monomohan Dass, Arun Chandra Guha, Lakshmi Kanta Maitra, Mihir Lal Chattopadhyay, Satis Chandra Samanta, Suresh Chandra Majumdar, Upendranath Barman, Prabhudayal Himatsingka, Basanta Kumar Das, Mrs. Renuka Ray, H.C. Mookherjee, Surendra Mohan Ghose, Syama Prasad Mookerjee, Ari Bahadur Gurung, R.E. Patel, K.C. Neogy, Raghib Ahsan, Somnath Lahiri, Jasimuddin Ahmad, Naziruddin Ahmad, Abdul Hamid Abdul Halim Ghuznavi

United Provinces: Ajit Prasad Jain, Algu Rai Shastri, Balkrishna Sharma, Banshi Dhar Misra, Bhagwan Din, Damodar Swarup Seth, Dayal Das Bhagat, Dharam Prakash, A. Dharam Dass, R.V. Dhulekar, Feroz Gandhi, Gopal Narain, Krishna Chandra Sharma, Govind Ballabh Pant, Govind Malaviya, Har Govind Pant, Harihar Nath Shastri, Hriday Nath Kunzru, Jaspat Roy Kapoor, Jagannath Baksh Singh, Jawaharlal Nehru, Jogendra Singh, Jugal Kishore, Jwala Prasad Srivastava, B.V. Keskar,

Mrs. Kamala Chaudhri, Kamalapati Tiwari, J.B. Kripalani, Mahavir Tyagi, Khurshed Lal, Masurya Din, Mohan Lal Saksena, Padampat Singhania, Phool Singh, Paragi Lal, Mrs. Purnima Banerjee, Prurshottam Das Tandon, Hira Vallabha Tripathi, Ram Chandra Gupta, Shibban Lal Saxena, Satish Chandra, John Matthai, Mrs. Sucheta Kripalani, Sunder Lall, Venkatesh Narayan Tivary, Mohanlal Gautam, Vishwambhar Dayal Tripathi, Vishnu Sharan Dublish, Begum Aizaz Rasul, Hyder Hussain, Hasrat Mohani, Abul Kalam Azad, Muhammad Ismail Khan, Rafi Ahmad Kidwai, Mohd. Hifzur Rahman

East Punjab: Bakshi Tek Chand, Jairamdas Daulatram, Thakurdas Bhargava, Bikramlal Sondhi, Yashwant Rai, Ranbir Singh, Achint Ram, Nand Lal, Sardar Baldev Singh, Giani Gurmukh Singh Musafir, Sardar Hukam Singh, Sardar Bhopinder Singh Mann, Sardar Rattan Singh Lohgarh

Bihar: Amiyo Kumar Ghosh, Anugrah Narayan Sinha, Banarsi Prasad Jhunjhunwala, Bhagwat Prasad, Boniface Lakra, Brajeshwar Prasad, Chandika Ram, K.T. Shah, Devendra Nath Samanta, Dip Narain Sinha, Guptanath Singh, Jadubans Sahay, Jagat Narain Lal, Jagjivan Ram, Jaipal Singh, Kameshwara Singh of Darbhanga, Kamaleshwari Prasad Yadav, Mahesh Prasad Sinha, Krishna Ballabh Sahay, Raghunandan Prasad, Rajendra Prasad, Rameshwar Prasad Sinha, Ramnarayan Singh, Sachchidananda Sinha, Sarangdhar Sinha, Satyanarayan Sinha, Binodanand Jha, P.K. Sen, Sri Krishna Sinha, Sri Narayan Mahtha, Syamanandan Sahaya, Hussain Imam, Syed Jafar Imam, Latifur Rahman, Mohammad Tahir, Tajamul Hussain, Choudhry Abid Hussain, Pt. Hargovind Mishra.

Central Provinces and Berar: Raghu Vira, Rajkumari Amrit Kaur, B.A. Mandloi, Brijlal Nandlal Biyani, Thakur Cheedilal, Seth Govind Das, Hari Singh Gour, Hari Vishnu

Kamath, Hemchandra Jagobaji Khandekar, Ghanshyam Singh Gupta, Lakshman Shrawan Bhatkar, Panjabrao Shamrao Deshmukh, Ravi Shankar Shukla, R.K. Sidhva, Shankar Trimbak Dharmadhikari, Frank Anthony, Kazi Syed Karimuddin, Ganpatrao Dani

Assam: Nibaṛan Chandra Laskar, Dharanidhar Basu-Matari, Gopinath Bardoloi, J.J.M. Nichols-Roy, Kuladhar Chaliha, Rohini Kumar Chaudhury, Muhammad Saadulla, Abdur Rouf

Orissa: B. Das, Biswanath Das, Krishna Chandra Gajapati Narayana Deo of Parlakimedi, Harekrushna Mahatab, Laxminarayan Sahu, Lokanath Misra, Nandkishore Das, Rajkrishna Bose, Santanu Kumar Das, Yudhishir Mishra

Delhi: Deshbandhu Gupta

Ajmer: Merwara Mukut Bihari Lal Bhargava

Coorg: C.M. Poonacha

Mysore: K.C. Reddy, T. Siddalingaiya, H.R. Guruv Reddy, S.V. Krishnamurthy Rao, K. Hanumanthaiya, H. Siddaveerappa, T. Channiah

Jammu and Kashmir: Sheikh Muhammad Abdullah, Motiram Baigra, Mirza Mohmmad Afzal Beg, Maulana Mohammad Sayeed Masoodi

Travancore-Cochin: Pattom A. Thanu Pillai

Madhya Bharat: Vinayak Sitaram Sarwate, Brijraj Narain, Gopikrishna Vijayavargiya, Ram Sahai, Kusum Kant Jain, Radhavallabh Vijayavargiya, Sitaram S. Jajoo

Saurashtra: Balwant Rai Gopalji Mehta, Jaisukhlal Hathi, Amritlal Vithaldas Thakkar, Chimanlal Chakubhai Shah, Samaldas Laxmidas Gandhi

Rajasthan: V.T. Krishnamachari, Hiralal Shastri, Sardar Singhjhi of Khetri, Jaswant Singhji, Raj Bhadur, Manikya Lal Varma, Gokul Lal Asava, Ramchandra Upadhyaya, Balwant Sinha Mehta, Dalel Singh, Jainarain Vyas

Patiala and East Punjab States Union: Ranjit Singh, Sochet Singh, Bhagwant Roy

Bombay States: Vinayakrao Balshankar Vaidya, B.N. Munavalli, Gokulbhai Daulatram Bhatt, Jivraj Narayan Mehta, Gopaldas A. Desai, Paranlal Thakurlal Munshi, B.H. Khardekar, Ratnappa Bharamappa Kumbhar

Orissa States: Lal Mohan Pati, N. Madhava Rau, Raj Kunwar, Sarangadhar Das, Yudhishthir Misra

Central Provinces States: R.L. Malaviya, Kishorimohan Tripathi, Ramprasad Potai

United Provinces States: B.H. Zaidi, Krishna Singh

Madras States: V. Ramaiah

Vindhya Pradesh: Avdesh Pratap Singh, Shambu Nath Shukla, Ram Sahai Tiwari, Mannulalji Diwedi

Cooch Behar: Himmat Singh K. Maheshwari

Tripura and Manipur: Girja Shankar Guha

Bhopal: Lal Singh

Kutch Bhawani: Arjun Khimji

Himachal Pradesh: Yashwant Singh Parmar.

Chapter VII

Goodwill Messages from Abroad on the Opening Day of the Constituent Assembly and the Inaugural Address by Sachchidananda Sinha, Provisional Chairman

As Scheduled, the first meeting of the Constituent Assembly duly opened on Monday, December 9, 1946, at 11 A.M. The first item on the agenda was that of the election of the temporary Chairman. Accordingly, at the outset, Sh. J.B. Kripalani, then Congress President, stood up to request Sachchidananda Sinha – the oldest member – to take the Chair as temporary Chairman.

The following goodwill messages were received from Governments abroad on the said auspicious occasion:—

(a) **From the United States**: With the approach of December 9, I extend to you as Provisional Chairman of the Constituent Assembly, and through you to the Indian people, the sincere good wishes of the United States Government and of the people of the United States for a successful conclusion of the great task you are about to undertake. India has a great contribution to make to the peace, stability, and cultural advancement of mankind, and your deliberations will be watched with deep interest and hope by freedom-loving people throughout the entire world.

(b) **From the Republic of China**: On the auspicious occasion of the opening of the Indian Constituent Assembly I have the honour to extend to Your Excellency in the name of the National Government of China my heartiest congratulations. I sincerely hope that your great Assembly succeeds in laying a solid foundation for a democratic and prosperous India.

(c) **From Australia**: Australia has watched with keen interest and sympathy the course of events which have given the people of India their rightful place in the community of nations. The Australian Government, therefore, greets the opening of the Constituent Assembly as an outward sign of a new era for India and offers the delegates of the Constituent Assembly their best wishes for success in their task.

The inaugural speech by Sachchidananda Sinha, the Provisional Chairman. The Chairman opened his remarks in the following manner:—

> "I am deeply beholden to you for your having agreed to accept me as the first President of your Constituent Assembly, which will enable me to assist you in transacting the preliminary business before the House – such as the election of permanent President, the framing of the Rules of Business, the appointment of various committees, and settling the question of giving publicity to, or keeping confidential, your proceedings – which will ultimately lead you to crown your labours by formulating a suitable and stable Constitution for an Independent India."

The Chairman made the following observations about the Constituent Assembly:—

> "This political method of devising a constitution for a country has not been known to our fellow-subjects in Britain, for the simple reason, that under

the British Constitution, there is no such thing as a constituent law, it being a cherished privilege of the British Parliament, as the sole sovereign authority, to make and unmake all laws, including the constitutional law of the country. As such, we have to look to countries other than British to be able to form a correct estimate of the position of a Constituent Assembly. In Europe, the oldest Republic that of Switzerland, has not had a Constituent Law, in the ordinary sense of that term, for it came into existence, on a much smaller scale than it now exists, due to historic causes and accidents, several centuries back."

The Chairman then referred to the Constitution of Switzerland and recommended the same in the following manner:—

"Switzerland has several notable and instructive features, which have strongly been recommended by qualified authorities to Indian Constitution-makers, and I have no doubt that this great Assembly will study carefully the Swiss Constitution, and try to utilize it to the best advantage in the interest of preparing a suitable constitution for a free and independent India."

The Chairman then referred to the first Constituent Assembly of France called "French National Assembly." The President then referred to the fact that "the French constitution-makers, who met in 1789 at the first Constituent Assembly of their country, were themselves largely influenced by the work done but a couple of years earlier, in 1787, by the historic Constitutional Convention held at Philadelphia by the American Constitution-makers for their country."

The President then referred to the great Constitution of the United States of America in the following manner:—

> "It is this great Constitution, which had been naturally taken as the model for all subsequent Constitutions not only of France, but also of the self-governing Dominions of the British Commonwealth, like Canada, Australia, and South Africa; and I have no doubt that you will also, in the nature of things, pay in the course of your work, greater attention to the provisions of the American Constitution than to those of any other."

The Chairman then referred to the Canadian Constitution which was drawn in 1864 in Quebec. Thereafter the Chairman referred to the Constitutions of Australia and South Africa in the following manner:—

> "The American Constitutional system was more or less adopted in the schemes prepared for framing the Constitutions of Australia and South Africa, which shows that the results achieved by the American Convention, held at Philadelphia in 1787, had been accepted by the world as a model for framing independent federal Constitution for various countries."

The Chairman commended to the Assembly for careful consideration and acceptance, with reasonable agreements and judicious compromises, the fundamental principles of the American system.

The Chairman then quoted the British authority, namely Viscount Bryce, and the American Jurist Joseph Story and also James who was at one time Solicitor-General of the United States.

Having made reference to the Constitution of America, Europe, and the South Africa, the President then referred to the constitutional aspects in this country and he first referred to the statement of Mahatma Gandhi made as far back as in 1922 in the following manner:—

"Swaraj will not be a free gift of the British Parliament. It will be a declaration of India's full self-expression, expressed through an Act of Parliament. But it will be merely a courteous ratification of the declared wish of the people of India. The ratification will be a treaty to which Britain will be a party. The British Parliament, when the settlement comes, will ratify the wishes of the people of India as expressed through the freely chosen representatives."

The statement made by Mahatma Gandhi was affirmed from time-to-time by various public bodies and political leaders.

The Chairman then referred to the session of the Congress held at Faizpur in December, 1936 which confirmed the earlier resolution in the following manner:—

"The Congress stands for a genuine democratic State in India where political power has been transferred to the people, as a whole, and the Government is under their effective control. Such a State can only come into existence through a Constituent Assembly having the power to determine finally the Constitution of the Country."

The Chairman referred to the Congress Working Committee Resolution in November, 1939, which declared that "Recognition of India's independence and the right of her people to frame their Constitution through a Constituent assembly is essential."

The Chairman ended his speech in the following manner:—

"I wish your labour success, and invoke Divine blessings that your proceedings may be marked not only by good sense, public spirit, and genuine patriotism, but also by wisdom, tolerance, justice, and fairness to all; and above all with a vision which may restore India to her pristine glory, and give her a place of honour and equality amongst the great nations of the world. Let us not forget to justify the pride of the great Indian poet, Iqbal, and his faith in the immortality of the destiny of our great, historic, and ancient country, when he summed up in these beautiful lines:

Yunan-o-Misr-o-Rome sab mit gaye jahan se,
Baqi abhi talak hai nam-o-nishan hamare.
Kuch bat hai ke hasti mit-ti-nahin hamari,
Sadion raha hai dushman daur-e-zaman hamara.

Pages 393 to 401: The Framing of India's Constitution – Select Documents (Vol. 1) by B. Shiva Rao.

Chapter VIII
The Objectives' Resolution (Dec. 1946 – Jan. 1947) – Pandit Nehru's Speech and the Speech of Dr. S. Radhakrishnan

The Experts' Committee appointed by the Indian National Congress for preparing material for the Constituent Assembly decided on July 20-22, 1946, that in the first session of the Constituent Assembly, after the appointment of an advisory committee on fundamental rights, etc. a resolution outlining the main objectives of the Constituent Assembly should be moved.

When the Constituent Assembly met on 9th December, 1946 one of the earliest tasks to which it addressed itself was to declare the basic objectives and guiding principles to be kept in view in the process of Constitution-making. This was achieved by the historic Objectives' Resolution moved by Nehru on December 13, four days after the first sitting of the Assembly. The draft of the resolution, which closely followed the text adopted by the Congress Experts' Committee, was approved by the Working Committee of the Congress, meeting a day before the first meeting of the Constituent assembly. The Assembly discussed it for five days.

The resumed discussion lasted three more days – January 20-22, 1947. On the last day it was adopted unanimously and in a solemn manner by all members standing. Following are the salient features of the text of the Resolution:—

(1) This Constituent Assembly declares its firm and solemn resolve to proclaim India as an Independent, Sovereign Republic and to draw up for her future governance a Constitution;

(2) Wherein all power and authority of the Sovereign Independent India, its constituent parts and organs of Government, are derived from the people;

(3) Wherein shall be guaranteed and secured to all the people of India justice, social, economic and political; equality of status, of opportunity, and before the law; freedom of thought, expression, belief, faith, worship; vocation, association and action, subject to law and public morality;

(4) Wherein adequate safeguards shall be provided for minorities, backward and tribal areas, and depressed and other backward classes;

(5) Whereby shall be maintained the integrity of the territory of the Republic and its sovereign rights on land, sea, and air according to justice and the law of civilized nations; and

(6) This ancient land attains its rightful and honoured place in the world and makes its full and willing contribution to the promotion of world peace and the welfare of mankind.

Nehru's Speech on the Resolution

Pandit Nehru referred to the work pending before the first session of the Constituent Assembly, where the Assembly had to pass the Rules of Procedure, and to appoint Committees, before proceeding to the real steps to the real work of the Constituent Assembly. Placing the Resolution, he further said as under:—

"But even now, at this stage, it is surely desirable that we should give some indication to ourselves, to those who look to this Assembly, to those millions in this country who are looking up to us and to the world at large, as to what we may do, what we seek to achieve, whither we are going. It is with this purpose that I have placed this Resolution before this House. It is a Resolution and yet, it is something much more than a resolution. It is a Declaration. It is a firm resolve. It is a pledge and an undertaking and it is for all of us, I hope, a dedication. And I wish this House, if I may say so respectfully, should consider this Resolution not in a spirit of narrow legal wording, but rather look at the spirit behind that Resolution. Words are magic things often enough, but even the magic of words sometimes cannot convey the magic of the human spirit and of a Nation's passion.

I venture to place this Resolution before the House and it is in that spirit that I trust the House will receive it and ultimately pass it. And may I, Sir, also, with all respect, suggest to you and to the House that, when the time comes for the passing of this Resolution let it be not done in the formal way by the raising of hands, but much more solemnly, by all of us standing up and thus taking this pledge anew."

He further said as under:—

"Nevertheless, the time comes when we have to rise above party and think of the Nation, think sometimes of even the world at large of which our Nation is a great part. And when I think of the work of this Constituent Assembly, it seems to me, the time has come when we should, so far as we are capable of it, rise above our ordinary selves and party disputes and think of the great problem before us in the widest and most tolerant and most effective manner so that, whatever we may produce, should be worthy of India as a whole and should be such that the world should recognize that we have functioned, as we should have functioned, in this high adventure.

As I stand here, Sir, I feel the weight of all manner of things crowding around me. We are at the end of an era and possibly very soon we shall embark upon a new age, and my mind goes back to the great past of India, to the 5,000 years of India's history, from the very dawn of that history which might be considered almost the dawn of human history, till today.

I think also of the various Constituent Assemblies that have gone before and of what took place at the making of a great American nation when the father of that nation met and fashioned out a Constitution which has stood the test of so many years, more than a century and a half, and of the great nation which has resulted, which has been built up on the basis of that Constitution.

Then my mind goes back to a more recent revolution which gave rise to a new type of State, the revolution that took place in Russia and out of which has arisen the Union of the Soviet Socialist Republics, another mighty country which is playing a tremendous part in the world, not only a mighty country but for us in India, a neighbouring country.

We may improve upon it. In any event whatever system of Government we may establish here must fit in with the temper of our people and be acceptable to them. We stand for democracy. It will be for this House to determine what shape to give to that democracy, the fullest democracy.

Others might take objection to this Resolution on the ground that we have not said that it should be a Socialist State. Well, I stand for Socialism and, I hope, India will stand for Socialism and that India will go towards the Constitution of a Socialist State and I do believe that the whole world will have to go that way."

He ended his speech with the following words:—

"Well, Sir, we are going to make a Constitution for India and it is obvious that what we are going to do in India, is going to have a powerful effect on the rest of the world, not only because a new free independent nation comes out into the arena of the world, but because of the very fact that India is such a country that by virtue, not only of her large size and population, but of her enormous resources and her ability to exploit those resources, she can immediately play an important and vital part in world affairs. Even today, on the verge of freedom as we are today, India has begun to play an important part in world affairs. Therefore, it is right that the framers of our Constitution should always bear this larger international aspect in mind.

In this Constituent Assembly we are functioning on a world stage and the eyes of the world are upon us and the eyes of our entire past are upon us. Our past is witness to what we are doing here and though the future is still unborn, the future too somehow looks at us, I think, and so, I would beg of this House to consider this Resolution in this mighty prospect of our past, of the turmoil of the present and of the great and unborn future that is going to take place soon. Sir, I beg to move......"

Radhakrishnan's Speech

Mr. Chairman, Sir, I have great pleasure in commending this Resolution to the acceptance of the House. From the list of amendments tabled, I see that there are three different questions raised: whether a declaration of this character is essential; whether this is the proper time for considering such a declaration; and whether objectives included in this Resolution are matters of general agreement or they require modification or amendment.

He further said "We" cannot say that the republican tradition is foreign to the genius of this country. We have had it from the beginning of our history. When a few merchants from the north, went down to the south, one of the Princes of Deccan asked the question, "who is your King?" The answer was, "some of us are governed by assemblies, some of us by kings."

He further said that we are actors today in a great historical drama. We are involved in it and therefore we are unable to perceive the large contours of it. This declaration, which we make today, is of the nature of a pledge to our own people and a pact with the civilized world.

He ended his speech with the following words:—

> "Here are the two alternatives. Accept the Constituent Assembly. Take its findings. Find out whether there are adequate safeguards for minorities or not. If they are there, give them the force of law and you may get co-operation."

The Objective Resolution was the foundation of the framing of the Constitution, as reflected in its Preamble.

Preamble as finally adopted by the Constitutent Assembly reads as under:

> "WE, THE PEOPLE OF INDIA, having solemnly resolved to constitute India into a SOVEREIGN SOCIALIST SECULAR DEMOCRATIC REPUBLIC and to secure to all its citizens:
> JUSTICE, social, economic and political;
> LIBERTY of thought, expression, belief, faith and worship;
> EQUALITY of status and of opportunity;
> and to promote among them all
> FRATERNITY assuring the dignity of the individual and the unity and integrity of the Nation"

The Framing of India's Constitution – Select Documents (Vol. 2) by B. Shiva Rao, pp. 1 to 18.

Chapter IX
The Questionnaire Issued by the Constitutional Adviser – March 17, 1947

To understand the scope and functioning of the various committees formed by the constituent assembly, it is essential to examine the questionnaire issued by the Constitutional Adviser, Shri B.N. Rau to the members of the Union Constitutional Committee and the Provincial Constitutional Committees. The colossal work required by the Committees in framing the Constitution of India is best demonstrated by the questionnaire issued by the Constitutional Adviser. The broad concept and parameters to be kept in view while making the Constitution is best seen by the questionnaire which runs in 4 parts. The questionnaire along with short notes appended are given hereinbelow and the questionnaire shows the amplitude of the work undertaken by the Constitutional Adviser.

QUESTIONNAIRE

A: HEAD OF THE INDIAN UNION

1. What should be the designation of the Head of the Indian Union?

References were made to the Constitutions of USA, Switzerland, Ireland, Canada, Australia and South Africa.

USA, Switzerland & Ireland-President.

Canada, Australia – The local Executive Head is the Governor-General on behalf of His Majesty.

2. How should be chosen?

Herein again references were made to the Constitution of USA, Switzerland and Ireland.

The answer will probably turn on whether the Head of the Indian Union is to be a real Head as in the U.S.A. or merely a nominal Head as in Switzerland. If he is to be a nominal head, not independent of the legislature as in Switzerland.

3. What should be his term of office?

References were made to the following countries:

(1) USA – 4 years (elected every leap year)

(2) Switzerland – 1 year (annual election)

(3) Ireland – 7 years

(4) Canada – Customary term of 5 years.

(5) Australia

(6) South Africa

The answer will probably be Customary term of 5 years.

4. Should he be eligible for re-election?

References were made to the Constitutions of USA, Switzerland and Ireland.

5. Should the office rotate among the different committees in turn? If so, how?

References were again made to the Constitutions of USA, Switzerland and Ireland.

6. Assuming that the Indian Union is to have a President as its Head, should there be a Vice-President or Vice-Presidents?

Reference was made to the provisions in the Constitutions of **USA, Switzerland, Ireland and USSR.**

7. What should be the term of office of a Vice-President?

Examples were given of the Constitutions of USA, Switzerland and Ireland.

USA – 4 years (election every leap year)

Switzerland – 1 year.

Ireland – No Vice-President.

8. What should be the functions of the President?

The functions of the Presidents given in the Constitutions of USA, Switzerland and Ireland were considered.

9. What should be the functions of the Vice-President?

References were made to the Constitutions of USA and Ireland.

10. Should the President be liable to be removed? If so, in what manner?

Reference was made to the Constitutions of USA, Switzerland and Ireland.

USA – The President is removable from office only by impeachment. The Lower Chamber initiates proceedings and the Senate sits as a court of trial. The President is removed on the majority vote of the Senate sitting as the court of impeachment.

Switzerland – No specific provision.

Ireland – Removable by impeachment. The President may be impeached for stated misbehaviour. A proposal to either House to prefer a charge against the President is entertained when moved in writing by at least 30 members of that House and is adopted when at least two-thirds of the total members support it. The other House investigates the charges or causes the charges to be investigated. If it sustains the charge by a two-thirds majority of the total members, the President is removed.

11. How is a temporary vacancy in the office of the President to be filled?

References were made to the Constitutions of USA, Switzerland and Ireland.

USA – The Vice-President acts as President for the rest of the term.

Switzerland – Apparently the Vice-President acts as President.

Ireland – A commission consisting of the Chief Justice, the Chairman of Dail Eireann and the Chairman of Senate acts for the President. The Commission may act by any two of their numbers.

The above questionnaire relating to the head of the Indian Union shows that a great comparison was made with various Constitutions of the world, as to the powers, mode of appointment, terms of the President and even how the President is to be removed in various countries.

QUESTIONNAIRE

B: EXECUTIVE

12. What should be the nature and type of the Union Executive? Should it be of the British type (Parliamentary) or the American type (non-Parliamentary) or the Swiss type (mixed) or any other type.

References were made to the Constitutions of USA and the Dominions, USA, Switzerland and Ireland.

U.K. and the Dominions – By convention the Executive (Cabinet) is responsible to the Legislature and retains office so long as it enjoys the confidence of the Legislature.

USA – The President is the head of the Federal Executive with a Cabinet of 10 heads of departments called Secretaries, appointed by him, subject to the nominal approval of the Senate and answerable only to him. Executive not responsible to Legislature. Non-Parliamentary.

Switzerland – The Federal Council consists of 7 members elected by the Legislature (by proportional representation) once in 4 years. They are eligible for re-election. Not more than one is elected from the same Canton. A mixture of Parliamentary and non-Parliamentary.

Ireland – Ireland has put into statutory form what in U.K. is based on convention. The government consists of 76 to 15 members appointed by the President. One of them acts as Prime Minister, and another as Deputy Prime Minister. Responsible to Dail Eireann, though the Ministers may be chosen from both the Houses, at most two from the Senate. Parliamentary.

13. If Parliamentary, should there be any special provision to secure a stable Executive?

References were made to the observations of Simon-Attlee Report in which the Constitutions of Ireland and China were considered.

14. What should be the composition of the Executive? What should be the maximum, if any, the number of Ministers?

References were made to the Constitutions of U.K., Canada, Australia, South Africa, USA, Switzerland and Ireland.

UK – No statutory maximum. The number at present in the Cabinet is 20 members including the Prime Minister.

Canada – No statutory maximum; the number at present is 20 members including the Prime Minister.

Australia – There is a statutory maximum of seven until Parliament otherwise provides. The number at present is 19 members including the Prime Minister. Ministers cannot remain in office for more than 3 months without being members of one of the Houses of the Legislature.

South Africa – There is a statutory maximum of eleven. Ministers cannot remain in office for more than 3 months without being members of one of the Houses of the Legislature.

USA – President with 10 heads of departments called Secretaries who are answerable only to him. None of these can be a member of either House of the Legislature.

Switzerland – The Federal Council consists of 7 members elected by the two Houses of the Legislature at a joint sitting. None of them can be a member of either House, but all may sit and speak without voting.

Ireland – Consists of 7 to 15 Ministers, selected from among the members of both the Houses, not more than two being selected from the Upper House. All continue to be members of the House from which they were selected.

15. Should provision be made to secure representation of different communities on the Executive? If so, how?

References were made to provisions existing in the Constitutions of USA, and Canada.

16. How should joint responsibility or co-ordination be secured?

References were made to the Constitutions of U.K. and the Dominions, USA, Switzerland and Ireland.

17. How should the members of the Executive be chosen?

UK and the Dominions: The choice of the Prime Minister is made by the King, or the Governor-General, as the case may be, and the nature of the choice depends upon the state of parties in the Lower House. The Prime Minister chooses his colleagues in the Cabinet.

U.S.A.: President (elected by an electoral college) selects his Secretaries subject to the normal approval of the Senate.

Switzerland: The members of the Federal Council chosen by the Federal Legislature at a joint sitting.

Ireland: The President appoints the Prime Minister on the recommendation of Dail Eireann and other Ministers on the recommendation of Prime Minister.

18. What provisions should be made for the removal of the Executive?

Again references were made to the provisions existing in the Constitutions of U.K. and the Dominions, USA, Switzerland and Ireland.

UK and the Dominions – The Cabinet holds office so long as it has the confidence of the Lower House. It can be removed by a vote of no-confidence by the Lower House.

USA – President may be removed by impeachment; Secretaries are removable by the President.

Switzerland – No specific provision.

Ireland – The Prime Minister and Ministers hold office so long as they have the support of the majority in the Lower House. Individual Ministers can be removed from office on the advice of the Prime Minister.

19. What should be the nature of relations between the Head of the Union and the Executive?

References were made to the Constitutions of U.K. and the Dominions, USA, Switzerland and Ireland.

UK – The King is merely a formal Head. In all political matters he acts on the advice of the Cabinet. He has prerogative powers namely, (1) the right to dissolve Parliament, (2) the right to refuse a dissolution of Parliament, and (3) the right to select Prime Minister. These rights are circumscribed by many considerations and are very often of theoretical interest only. There are also certain personal prerogatives which he exercises on his own responsibility.

Dominions – The Cabinet is the *de facto* Executive. In all political matters the Governor-General acts on the advise of the Cabinet. He does not preside over the business meetings of the Cabinet, which are summoned in the name of the Prime Minister. The Governor-General acts merely as the constitutional head of the Government advised by the Ministers.

USA – The President is the Head of the Union, as well as the Chief Executive.

Switzerland – The President is the Head of the Union and also a Minister-in-charge of an administrative department like other Ministers. No special powers, except those of formal or ceremonial character, vested in him.

Ireland – The President is the titular head and all laws are promulgated in his name. The President acts with the consent of the Prime Minister and his Cabinet except when the Cabinet loses the confidence of the Dail. In that case the President may in his discretion, dissolve the Dail and call for fresh elections. The President is also advised by the Council of State which has the Minister and Deputy Prime Minister among its members.

QUESTIONNAIRE

C: LEGISLATURE

20. Should the Union Legislature have a single Chamber or two Chambers?

U.K and the Dominions: All bicameral

(Two Chambers)

U.K. – House of Lords (Upper House)

Canada – Senate (Upper House)

House of Commons (Lower House)

Australia – Senate (Upper House, House of Representatives (Lower House)

South Africa – Senate (Upper House), House of Assembly (Lower House)

USA – Bicarneral: Senate (Upper House), and House of Representatives (Lower House)

Switzerland: Bicameral: Council of States (Upper House), and National Council (Lower House)

Ireland: Bicameral: Senate Eireann (Upper House), and Dail Eireann (Lower House).

21. What provisions should be made for the adequate representation of different communities and interests?

U.K: Universities are given special representation.

South Africa: 4 elected and 4 nominated to represent native interests in the Upper House. 3-seats allotted in the Lower House for natives of Cape Colony.

USA: No provision.

Switzerland: No specific provision. The system of proportional representation helps to secure the adequate representation of different communities.

Ireland: Provision made for the representation of functional interests such as "agricultural and allied interests and fisheries", "Labour", Industry and Commerce" in the Upper House; system of proportional representation for the Lower House.

22. What should be the term of the Union Legislature?

UK: Upper House: largely hereditary. Lower House: 5 years, unless sooner dissolved.

Canada: Upper House: Senators are nominated for life. Lower House: 5 years.

Australia: Upper House: Continuous, half retiring every three years, term of members being six years. Lower House: 3 years.

USA: Lower House: Two years, Upper House: Continuous, one-third retiring every two years, term of membership being six years.

Switzerland: Lower House: 4 years. Upper House: Each Canton or half-Canton free to fix the term of office of its representatives. Varies from 1 to 4 years.

Ireland: Lower House: 7 years, unless sooner dissolved. A shorter period may be fixed by law. Upper House: Same as for Lower House.

QUESTIONNAIRE

D: JUDICIARY

23. Should there be a separate chain of courts to administer Union Laws?

In USA there is a separate chain of Federal Courts, but not in Canada, Australia or Switzerland.

USA: Under the Constitution the judicial power of the United States is vested in a Supreme Court, and in such inferior courts as the Congress may from time-to-time ordain and establish. There are, at present, two sets of inferior federal Courts, namely, the Federal District Courts and the Circuit Courts of Appeal. The country is divided into 83 districts, each State constituting at least one district. From the Federal Courts of these districts there is an appeal to Circuit Courts, which are ten in number. There are also two special courts, namely the Court of Claims and the Court of Customs Appeals.

Australia: The judicial power of the Commonwealth is vested in a Federal Supreme Court, called the High Court of Australia, and "in such other federal courts as the Parliament creates, and in such other courts as other federal courts as it invests with federal jurisdictions". The Parliament is also empowered to make laws investing any court of a State with federal jurisdiction.

Canada: Under the constitution the Canadian Parliament is empowered to establish a General Court of Appeal for Canada and other courts for the better administration of the laws of Canada. In the exercise of these powers, the Canadian Parliament has set up a Supreme Court of Appeal and an Exchequer court. In other respects, the administration of justice, including the

Constitution, maintenance and organization of civil and criminal courts and civil procedure, is a Provincial subject while criminal law and procedure are assigned to the Federation.

QUESTIONNAIRE

E: AMENDMENT TO CONSTITUTIONS

24. What provisions should be made regarding amendments to the Constitution?

Canada: The Constitution of the Dominion of Canada can only be amended by the Parliament of Great Britain. The Constitution Act itself does not contain any provision regarding such amendments and the Statute of Westminster clearly lays down that it should not be deemed to apply to the repeal, amendment or alteration of the "British North America Acts".

Australia: A proposal to amend the Constitution must be passed by an absolute majority in each of the two Houses, and not less than 2 or more than 6 months after its passage through both Houses, must be submitted in each State to the electors of the House of Representatives (Lower House). But if an amendment proposed by an absolute majority of one House is not agreed to by the other House and if after an interval of three months, the amendment is again proposed by the first-mentioned House and again not agreed to by the other House, the Governor-General may submit the proposed amendment to the electors in each State. The proposed amendment cannot become law unless it is approved by a majority of electors voting and by a majority of the States.

Union of South Africa: Except in regard to certain "entrenched" provisions the Union Parliament may by law repeal or alter any of the provisions of the Constitution Act. As regards the excepted provisions, *viz*. Section 35 (protection of the Cape native franchise).

USA: In the Constitution of the United States, two methods of originating amendments are provided, and there are also two methods of enacting amendments, when so originated. In the first place, Congress itself may, by a two-thirds majority in each House, draft and propose amendments; in the second place in the legislatures of two-thirds of the several states may apply to Congress to call a convention for the purpose of proposing amendments. When amendments are proposed by Congress, or by a constitutional convention, they have to be submitted to the States, and ratified in three-fourths of the States, either by the State Legislature or by State Conventions specially elected in each State for the purpose.

Switzerland: There are several methods by which revisions of the Constitution may be originated and ratified. A total revision of the Constitution may be brought about in three different ways.

Ireland: Every proposal for amending the Constitution must be initiated in the Lower House as a Bill and after it is passed by both the Houses of the Legislature, submitted to the people for their decision. The Bill is held to have been approved by the people if the majority of the votes cast is in favour of its enactment, and it becomes law after it is signed and promulgated by the President in due form.

The Framing of India's Constitution – Select Documents (Vol. 2) by B. Shiva Rao, pages 433 to 451.

Chapter X
Ambedkar's Speech Moving the Draft Constitution in the Constituent Assembly - November 4, 1948

The Draft Constitution as settled by the Drafting Committee was introduced in the Constituent Assembly by Dr. B.R. Ambedkar, the Chairman of the Committee, on November 4, 1948. He moved for its consideration the same day, and in doing so drew attention to the important features of the Constitution and dealt with the criticisms levelled against it.

Dr. B.R. Ambedkar introduced the draft Constitution as settled by the Drafting Committee and moved that it be taken into consideration. The Chairman pointed out that the Drafting Committee was appointed by a resolution passed by the Constituent Assembly on August 29, 1947.

The Chairman pointed out that the Draft Constitution as it has emerged from the Drafting Committee is a formidable document. It contains 315 articles and 8 schedules. It must be admitted that the Constitution of no country could be found to be so bulky as the Draft Constitution. It should be difficult for those who have not gone through it to realize its salient and special features.

The Chairman presented the reports of the following three Committees appointed by the Constituent Assembly:—

"(1) Report of the Committee on Chief Commissioners' Provinces,

(2) Report of the Expert Committee on Financial Relations between the Union and the States, and

(3) Report of the Advisory Committee on Tribal Areas.

The Chairman pointed out as under:—

> "To turn to the main question. A student of constitutional law, if a copy of Constitution is placed in his hands, is sure to ask two questions. *Firstly*, what is the form of government that is envisaged in the Constitution; and *Secondly*, what is the form of the Constitution?"

The Chairman then pointed out that the American form of government is called the Presidential System of Government and what the Draft Constitution proposes is the Parliamentary system. The two are fundamentally different. Under the Presidential system of America, the President is the chief head of the executive. The administration is vested in him. Under the Draft Constitution the President occupies the same position as the King under the English Constitution. He is the head of the State but not of the Executive. He represents the nation but does not rule the nation.

The Chairman pointed out the differences between the Presidential System in America and the draft Constitution in the following manner:—

> "The Presidential system of America is based upon the separation of the Executive and the Legislature, so that the President and his Secretaries cannot be members of the Congress. The Draft Constitution does not recognize this doctrine. The Ministers under the Indian Union are members of Parliament."

The Chairman compared the American, Swiss and the British system in the following manner:—

> "The American and the Swiss systems give more stability but less responsibility. The British system on the other hand gives you more responsibility but less stability. The reason for this is obvious. The American Executive is a non-Parliamentary Executive in the Congress, while the British system is a Parliamentary Executive which means that it is dependent upon a majority in Parliament. Being a non-Parliamentary Executive, the Congress of the United States cannot dismiss the Executive."

The Chairman then turned to the other question *viz.* the form of the Constitution.

The Chairman pointed out the two principal forms of the Constitution in the following manner:—

> "Two principal forms of the Constitution are known to history – one is a unitary and the other federal. The essential characteristics of a unitary Constitution are: (1) the supremacy of the central polity, and (2) the absence of subsidiary sovereign polities. Contrariwise, a federal Constitution is marked (1) by the existence of a Central policy and subsidiary polities side-by-side, and (2) by each being sovereign in the field assigned to it. In the other words, federation means the establishment of a dual polity. The Draft Constitution is a federal Constitution inasmuch as it establishes what may be called a dual polity. This dual polity under the proposed periphery, each endowed with sovereign powers to be exercised in the field assigned to them respectively by the Constitution. This dual polity resembles the American Constitution."

The Chairman pointed out that the proposed Indian Constitution is a dual polity with a single citizenship. There is a only one citizenship for the whole of India. It is Indian citizenship. There is no State citizenship. Every

Indian has the same rights of citizenship; no matter in what State he resides. The Chairman further pointed out that on the other hand the Draft Constitution can be both unitary as well as federal according to the requirements of time and circumstances. In normal times, it is framed to work as a federal system. But in times of war it is so designed as to make it work as though it was a unitary system. Once the President issues a Proclamation which he is authorized to do under the provisions of Article 275, the whole scene can become transformed and the State becomes a unitary State. The Chairman then compared the draft Constitution to the Australian Constitution.

The Chairman then pointed two differences. First is the power given to Parliament to legislate on exclusively provincial subjects in normal times and I referred to articles 226, 227 and 229. The chairman then pointed out that the second means adopted to avoid rigidity and legalism is the provision related to the amendment of the Constitution. The provisions of the Constitution relating to the amendment of the Constitution divide the articles of the Constitution into two groups. In the one group are placed articles relating to (a) the distribution of legislative powers between the Centre and the States, (b) the representation of the States in Parliament, and (c) the powers of the courts. All other articles are placed in another group. Articles placed in the second group cover a very large part of the Constitution and can be amended by Parliament by a double majority, namely, a majority of not less than two-thirds of the members of each House present and voting and by a majority of the total membership of each House. The amendment of these articles does not require ratification by the States.

The Chairman pointed out that the Draft Constitution has sought to forge means and methods whereby India will have a federation and at the same time will have uniformity in all basic matters which are essential to maintain the unity of the country. The means adopted by the Draft Constitution are three:

(1) a single judiciary;

(2) uniformity in fundamental laws, civil and criminal; and

(3) a common all-India civil service to man important posts.

The Chairman further pointed out that the High Courts and the Supreme Court form one single integrated judiciary having jurisdiction and providing remedies in all cases arising under the Constitutional law, the civil law or the criminal law. This is done to eliminate all diversity in all remedial procedures. Canada is the only country which furnishes a close parallel. The Australian system is only an approximation. Care is taken to eliminate all diversity from laws which are the basis of civic and corporate life. The great Codes of Civil and Criminal Laws, such as the Civil Procedure Code, the Penal Code, the Criminal Procedure Code, the Evidence Act, the Transfer of Property Act, Laws of Marriage, Divorce, and Inheritance, are placed in the Concurrent List so that the necessary uniformity can always be preserved without impairing the federal system.

The Chairman pointed out that the Constitution provides that without depriving the States of their right to form their own civil services, there shall be an All-India Service recruited on an all-India basis with common qualifications with uniform scales of pay, and the members of which alone could be appointed to these strategic posts throughout the Union.

The Chairman then pointed out to the fundamental rights mentioned in the Draft Constitution and further pointed out that in the Draft Constitution the fundamental rights are followed by what are called, "Directive Principles". It is a novel feature in a Constitution framed for Parliamentary democracy. The only other Constitution framed for Parliamentary democracy which embodies such principles is that of the Irish Free State.

The Chairman ended his speech with the following remarks:

> "No Constitution is perfect and the Drafting Committee itself is suggesting certain amendments to improve the Draft Constitution. But the debates in the Provincial Assemblies give me courage to say that the Constitution as settled by the Drafting Committee is good enough to make in this country a start with. I feel that it is workable, it is flexible and it is strong enough to hold the country together both in peace time and in war time. Indeed, if I may say so, if things go wrong under the new Constitution, the reason will not be that we had a bad Constitution. What we will have to say is, that Man was vile. Sir, I move."

The Framing of India's Constitution – Select Documents (Vol. 4) by B. Shiva Rao, pages 419 to 436.

Chapter XI
Draft Constitution as Revised by the Drafting Committee – November 3rd, 1949

The clause-by-clause consideration of the Draft Constitution, taken up by the Constituent Assembly on November 15, 1948, was concluded on October 17, 1949. The Draft Constitution, with the amendments adopted by the Assembly, was then referred again to the Drafting Committee with instructions to carry out such renumbering of the articles, clauses and sub-clauses, such revision of punctuation and such revision and completion of the marginal notes as might be necessary, and to recommend such formal or consequential or necessary amendments to the Constitution as might be required.

The Draft Constitution as revised by the Drafting Committee contained 395 articles and eight schedules and was submitted to the President of the Constituent Assembly on November 3, 1949. In this Draft, where words were substituted or new words inserted, they were indicated in ITALICS and where words were omitted such omission was indicated in ASTERISKS.

Apart from the additions, deletions and amendments incorporated in the revised Draft, the Drafting Committee gave notice of some further amendments. Notice of amendments was also given by other members of the Assembly. All these amendments were considered by the Assembly on November 14, 15 and 16, and they were put to vote on November 16.

Letter forwarding the revised draft of the Constitution was forwarded on 3rd November, 1949 to the Hon'ble President of the Constituent Assembly of India, New Delhi duly signed by the members *viz.*

1. B.R. Ambedkar
2. N. Gopalaswami Ayyangar
3. A. Krishnaswami Ayyar
4. K.M. Munshi
5. Saiyed Mohd. Saadulla
6. T.T. Krishnamachari.

Inter-alia it was mentioned as under:—

"The changes that we have recommended in the Draft Constitution fall broadly under four categories:

1. The renumbering of articles, clauses and sub-clauses, and the revision of punctuation,
2. Formal and consequential alterations, such as the omission of the words "of this Constitution" the changes in the use of capital letters, the alteration of the reference to Ruler to "Rajpramukh",
3. Certain necessary alterations proposed for making the meaning of some of the articles clearer or for filling-up any lacuna in an article without making any substantial change in the content thereof;
4. Certain other necessary amendments, whether by way of addition of new articles or by way of revision of the existing articles to remedy the defects and omissions that the scrutiny of the Draft Constitution has revealed to us.

The members made various suggestions regarding articles, 5, 22 (old 15A), 31 (old 24), 34 (new), 77 (old 64) and 16 (old 146), 100 (old 80) and 189 (old 164). Regarding Articles 222, 365, 395 and 392 (old 330), the following suggestions are made:—

> "**Article 22 (new):** We have proposed the insertion of this new article to enable the President to transfer a judge of a High Court from one High Court to another. The present provision in the Constitution would not permit of any compensatory allowance being given to judges on such transfer. Power has accordingly been reserved to Parliament to determine by law the compensatory allowance to be paid in case they are so transferred, and, until Parliament so determines, to the President to fix by order the quantum of such allowance.
>
> **Article 365 (new):** In certain articles of the Constitution, such as articles 256 (old 233), 257 (old 234 and 234-A), 353 (old 276), 360 (old 280-A) and 371 (old 306-B), power has been given to the Government of India to give directions to the States in various matters, and in some of these articles it has been mentioned that the failure to give effect to those directions will be deemed to be a failure to carry on the Government of the State in accordance with the provisions of the Constitution. We felt that this particular provision should be put in separate article and hence we have proposed the insertion of this new article.
>
> **Article 391:** It has been pointed out to us that there is a possibility of a further change being made in the territories of the States mentioned in the First Schedule, and that action in this direction might be taken under the existing provisions of the Government of India Act, 1935, between the passing of the Constitution and its commencement. It is therefore felt that authority should be given to the President to take cognizance of these changes on

the date when the Constitution comes into force and to make appropriate changes in the First and the Fourth Schedules. This article has accordingly been proposed to empower the President to take the necessary action.

Article 392 (old 313): A new clause (3) has been proposed for addition to this article giving power to the Governor-General to exercise the power of the President under this article in respect of the articles which will come into force on the passing of the Constitution and before its commencement.

Various changes were also suggested in the First and the Fourth Schedules and in List I, II and III.

As stated above, the letter forwarding the revised draft on 3rd November, 1949 was duly signed by the members *viz.* B.R. Ambedkar, N. Gopalaswami Ayyangar, A. Krishnaswamy Ayyar, K.M. Munshi, and Saiyed Mohd. Saadulla and T.T. Krishnamachari.

The text of the revised draft is available in pages 750-932- The Framing of India's Constitution – Select Documents (Vol. 4) by B. Shiva Rao.

Chapter XII
Constituent Assembly Rules of Procedure and Standing Orders
as Amended upto October 15, 1949

On December 21, 1946, K.M. Munshi presented to the Constituent Assembly the Report of the Committee on the Rules of Procedure. After clause-by-clause consideration of the Report for two days the Assembly finally adopted the rules recommended by the committee with certain amendments. The Rules were further amended from time-to-time and four editions were issued, the fourth edition having been issued in June 1949. The most important amendments were necessitated as a result of (a) partition of India and its effect on the Constituent Assembly, and (b) entry of the representatives of the Princely States. A few amendments were made even after June 1949.

THE FINANCE AND STAFF COMMITTEE—DECEMBER 23, 1946

The Constituent Assembly Rules of Procedure adopted by the House on December 23, 1946 provided *vide* rule 42, (rule 41 of the second, third and fourth editions of the Rules of Procedure) for the setting up of a Finance and Staff Committee for preparing the budget of the Assembly and for advising the President in regard to the Secretariat staff and the allowances of officers and members of the House and its Committees. Election to Committee was on December 23, 1946.

The following personnel were appointed to the Committee:—

Chairman: Rajendra Prasad, President of the Assembly.

Member: (1) H.C. Mookherjee, (2) V.T. Krishnamachari (Vice-Presidents of the Assembly), (3) Satyanarayan Singh, (4) Jaipal Singh, (5) V.I. Muniswami Pillai, (6) N.V. Gadgil, (7) Govind Das, (8) Sri Prakasha, (9) Rajkumari Amrit Kaur, (10) Bhawanji A. Khimji, and (11) K. Santhanam.

THE CREDENTIALS COMMITTEE—DECEMBER 23, 1946

Rules 43 and 44 (Nos. 42 and 43 in the second, third and fourth editions) of the Constituent Assembly. Rules of Procedure provided for the setting up of a Credential Committee for dealing with the credentials of the members of the Assembly. The Committee was to consist of five members who were to be elected by the House. It was first constituted on December 23, 1946. The personnel of the Committee and the text of the relevant rules are given below:

The following personnel were appointed to the Committee:

Chairman: Alladi Krishnaswami Ayyar.

Members: (1) P.K. Sen, (2) Bakshi Tek Chand, (3) B. Pocker, and (4) Ram Sahai.

THE HOUSE COMMITTEE—DECEMBER 23, 1946

The Constituent Assembly Rules of Procedure, *vide* Rule 45 (No. 4 in second, third and fourth editions) provided for the setting up of a House Committee to deal with the boarding, lodging and other problems of members during their stay at Delhi. The Committee was to consist of eleven members who were to be elected by the House. The Committee could co-opt more members and appoint sub-Committees. The Committee was elected on December 23, 1946. It appointed a sub-Committee on January 28, 1947 for advising on the actual allotment of accommodation to members.

The following personnel were appointed to the Committee and sub-Committee:—

Chairman: Pattabhi Sitaramayya.

Members: (1) Dip Narain Sinha, (2) Nand Kishore Das, (3) Mohan Lal Saxsena, (4) H.V. Kamath, (5) R.R. Diwakar, (6) Mrs. Ammu Swaminathan, (7) Mohd. Hassan, (8) Upendra Nath Barman, (9) Jainarayan Vyas, (10) B. Shiva Rao, and (11) Deshbandhu Gupta.

SUB-COMMITTEE

(1) B. Shiva Rao, (2) B. Pattabhi Sitaramayya, (3) Mohan Lal Saxsena, and (4) Deshbandhu Gupta.

THE STEERING COMMITTEE—JANUARY 21, 1947

Rules 40 and 41 of the Constituent Assembly Rules of Procedure (first Edition: in subsequent editions numbered as 39 and 40) provided for the election by the Assembly of eleven members to constitute a Steering Committee for arranging the order of business for the day, grouping similar motions and securing assent of the members to composite motions, and acting as a liason body between various wings, organs and functionaries of the Assembly. The President of the Assembly was to be the *ex-officio* chairman of the Committee and the Assembly could elect from time-to-time eight additional members. A resolution for the election of the committee was adopted by the House on January 20, 1947 and the elections were held the next day.

The following personnel were the members of the Committee:—

Chairman: Rajendra Prasad, President of the Assembly.

Members: (1) Sardar Vallabhbhai Patel, (2) Mrs. G. Durgabai, (3) S.H. Prater, (4) Satyanarayan Sinha, (5) M. Ananthasayanam Ayyangar, (6) K.M. Munshi, (7) Diwan Chaman Lal, (8) P. Govinda Menon, (9) C.S. Venkatachar, (10) Saiyed Mohd. Saadulla, (11) Abdul Kadar Mohd.

Shaikh, (12) Surendra Mohan Ghose, (13) Jagat Narain Lal, (14) J.B. Kripalani, (15) Gyani Gurmukh Singh Musafir, (16) K. Chengalvaraya Reddy, (17) Balwant Rai Mehta, (18) R.M. Nalvade, and (19) Suresh Chandra Mazumdar.

ORDER OF BUSINESS COMMITTEE—APRIL-JULY, 1947

On January 25, 1947, a resolution was moved in the Constituent Assembly by B. Pattabhi Sitaramayya for the setting up of a committee to recommend the order of future business of the House in regard to the framing of the Constitution. The Committee presided over by K.M. Munshi, submitted two reports. The first report was presented to the Assembly on April 30, 1947. In this report the Committee was not able to make final recommendations because of the fluid political circumstances issue and partition became a certainty. This brought about a great change in the programme of the Assembly inasmuch as some of the reports which had been submitted earlier required reconsideration in the light of later developments. The committee, in its final report presented on July 14, 1947, took note of these developments and stressed that the Assembly should complete its work by the end of October, 1947.

ADOPTION OF THE NATIONAL FLAG

The President of the Constituent Assembly appointed on June 23, 1947, under his Chairmanship an *ad hoc* committee to determine the National Flag of independent India. Besides the Chairman, the Committee consisted of Abdul Kalam Azad, C. Rajagopalachari, Shrimati Sarojini Naidu, K.M. Panikkar, K.M. Munshi, B.R. Ambedkar, Frank Anthony, B. Pattabhi Sitaramayya and four others.

July 22, on a motion by Pt. Jawaharlal Nehru the flag recommended by the Committee was finally adopted by the Assembly to be the National Flag of Independent India.

Dr. S. Radhakrishnan and Mohammad Saadullah who were amongst those who spoke on Nehru's motion, *inter alia,* explained the significance of the Flag with reference to the colour scheme adopted therein. Smt. Sarojini Naidu who was called upon by the President to make the last speech on the motion, concluded by making an eloquent appeal to the "men and women of re-born India" to rise and salute the flag; Nehru's motion was adopted, with the whole Assembly standing.

The Rules of Procedure have been given in the book "The Framing of India's Constitution – Select Documents by B. Shiva Rao (Volume I) from pages 437 to 491.

Chapter XIII

FUNDAMENTAL RIGHTS

The inclusion of a set of fundamental rights in India's Constitution had its genesis in the forces operating in the national struggle during British rule. With the resort by the British executive to such arbitrary acts as internments and deportations without trial and curbs on the liberty of the press in the early decades of this century, it became an article of faith with the leaders of the freedom movement.

In Pre-Independence India there was no charter of fundamental rights of a justiciable nature, and even such safeguards as were contained in the various statutes could be taken away by the authority making that statute, whether it was the British Parliament or a legislative authority in India. Moreover, there were in existence laws which, by the setting up of special courts or by curtailing a subject's rights and liberties, did violence to the basic principles of fundamental rights. The position was summed up by B.N. Rau in his report on Human Rights (December 1947). With a few exceptions, human rights in India today are not guaranteed by the Constitution.

By the Objective Resolution adopted on January 22, 1947, the Constituent Assembly solemnly pledged itself to draw up for India's future governance Constitution wherein "shall be guaranteed and secured to all the people of India Justice, social, economic and political, equality of status, of opportunity and before the law: freedom of thought, expression, belief, faith, worship, vocation, association and action, subject to law and public morality" and wherein adequate safeguards would be provided for minorities, backward and tribal areas and depressed and other classes. Two days after the adoption of the

Resolution, the Assembly elected an Advisory Committee for reporting on minorities, fundamental rights and on the tribal and excluded areas. The Advisory Committee in turn constituted on February 27, 1947, five sub-committees one of which was to deal with fundamental rights.

Before formulating its list of fundamental rights the sub-committee fully discussed the various drafts submitted by its members and others; the notes and memoranda – apart from those circulated by B.N. Rau – that received particular attention were those submitted by Alladi Krishnaswami Ayyar, K. M. Munshi and B.R. Ambedkar.

The draft report of the sub-committee completed on April 3, 1947, was circulated to its members with the explanatory notes on the various clauses prepared by B.N. Rau.

Sub-Committee on Minorities

Sub-Committee

Discussion in the constitution assembly of the draft provisions took place in November and December, 1948 and August, September and October 1949. During these meetings the Assembly considered various suggestions for amendment made on behalf of the Drafting Committee as well as those proposed by individual members of the Assembly. The provisions as passed by the Assembly were again scrutinized by the Drafting Committee and incorporated with drafting changes wherever necessary in the revised Draft Constitution. This revised Draft was again placed before the Assembly as its final session held in November 1949.

After discussing the subject of fundamental rights – described by Ambedkar as "the most critical part" of the Constitution – for as many as thirty-eight days in the sub-committee, two in the Advisory Committee and twenty-five in the Constituent Assembly – the Assembly ultimately adopted the comprehensive and impressive array of fundamental rights spread over twenty-two articles and divided broadly into seven categories of rights viz.,

(i) Right to equality
(ii) Right to freedom
(iii) Right against exploitation
(iv) Right to freedom of religion
(v) Cultural and educational rights
(vi) Right to property, and
(vii) Right to constitutional remedies.

Right to Equality (Draft Articles 14–18)

Equality before Law (Article 14)

Prohibition of Discrimination (Article 15)

Equality of employment opportunity (Article 16)

Abolition of Unthouchability (Article 17)

Abolition of Titles (Article 18)

The principle of guaranteeing to every person equality before law and equal protection of the laws was first included in the drafts submitted by Munshi and Ambedkar. Finally Munshi's draft with some modifications was adopted.

In an explanatory note, B.N. Rau pointed out that Equality before Law was widened so as to be applicable to all persons and not merely to citizens.

Alladi Krishnaswami Ayyar clarified that the clause as drafted made no discrimination of any sort between a citizen and a non-citizen even in matters like the exercise of trade, calling or profession.

At the stage of clause-by-clause consideration of the Draft Constitution the Assembly discussed draft article relating to Equality before Law and the equal protection of the laws and the draft article as proposed by the committee was accepted by the Assembly without any change.

Prohibition of the Discrimination (Draft Article 15)

The fundamental right guaranteeing that there would be no discrimination against any one on grounds of religion, race, colour, caste or sex, was embodied in the drafts submitted by Munshi and Ambedkar.

In his explanatory note, B.N. Rau mentioned that the above provision, generally followed the drafts in the Nehru Report (1928) and the Congress Declaration of 1933. Commenting on the draft, Alladi Krishnaswami Ayyar suggested *inter alia* that the provision forbidding discrimination might be made an independent clause. The Sub-Committee accepted his suggestions, and incorporated in its report to the Advisory Committee the non-discrimination provision as an independent clause.

When the Minorities Sub-Committee began to examine in detail the question of prohibition of discrimination at places of public resort, tanks, wells, etc., it realized that it might be necessary for the law to permit separate provision being made for women and children: likewise in public employment it was found necessary that reservation might have to be made for minorities. Munshi stated that the first sweeping generalization is practically inapplicable to the whole clause on prohibition of discrimination. He suggested that amendments should be examined by a small sub-committee or by the whole committee with these considerations in mind which was partly accepted. A sub-committee consisting of Munshi, Rajagopalachari, Panikkar and Ambedkar redrafted the clause which was finally accepted.

Various objections were raised by several members including Rajkumari Amrit Kaur, P.S. Deshmukh, Somanath Lahari, H.V. Kamath, Pattabhi Sitaramayya, R.K. Sidhva, Tajamul Husain, Mrs. Purnima Banerji,

Guptanath Singh, Jay Prakash Narayan, Sayed Abdur Rouf, Mahavir Tyagi, Mrs. G. Durgabai, Thakur Das Bhargava, T.T. Krishanmachari, K. Santhanam, Ananthya Sayanam Ayyangar, C. Subramaniyam, K.T. Shah, Momd. Tahir, S. Nagappa, Bhupinder Singh Mann, Shibbban Lal Saxena, & Rohini Kumar Choudhary but almost all these were rejected. However, some amendments made by C. Subramaniyam, Rouf and Guptanath Singh were accepted.

Equality of Employment Opportunity (Draft Article 16)

The principle of equality of opportunity and prohibition of discrimination on grounds of religion, race, colour, caste or language, in the matter of public employment, was contained in the drafts submitted by Munshi, Ambedkar, K.T. Shah and Harnam Singh. B.N. Rau stated that the sub-clause was adopted from the provisions of Govt. of India Act, 1935. The subsequent suggestion of Alladi Krishnaswami Ayyar was accepted and the provision was redrafted as an independent clause.

On an amendment moved by Munshi and accepted by Vallabhbhai Patel certain formal changes were made at this stage. Suggestions and objections were also made by Pattabhi Sitaramayya, R.R. Diwakar, S.V. Krishnamoorthy Rao, T.A. Ramalingam, Tajamul Husain, Upendranath Burman, Mrs. Purnima Banerji, Mohamed Tahir, Ananthasayanam Ayyangar, Jaspat Roy Kapoor, Alladi Krishnaswami Ayyar, Kamath, T.T. Krishnamachari, Loknath Misra, K.T. Shah, Hriday Nath Kunzru, Mohamed Ismail, K.M. Munshi, which were considered by the committee. The amendments proposed by Tahir, Ananthasayanam Ayyangar, Kapoor, Munshi, Alladi Krishnaswami Ayyar were accepted.

Abolition of Untouchability (Draft Article 17)

A clause providing for the abolition of the age-old social evil of "untouchability" was contained in Munshi's draft of Fundamental Rights. Other members who gave suggestions on this article included Jagjivan Ram, K.M. Panikkar, Rajagopalchari, H.V. Kamath, S. Nagappa, P. Kunhiraman, R.R. Diwakar, S.V. Krishnamoorthy Rao, Upendranath Barman, Naziruddin Ahmed, K.T. Shah, Muniswami Pillai, Manmohan Das, Santanu Kumar Das, Mrs. Dakshayani Velayudhan. These were considered appropriately by the committee and the article was finalized.

Abolition of Titles (Draft Article 18)

On April 30, 1947, during the consideration of this article in the Assembly, Vallabhbhai Patel observed that titles were "often being abused for corrupting the public life of the country", and that it was therefore better that their abolition should be provided as a fundamental right. Discussion took place in the Assembly on the suggestions made by speakers which included M.R. Masani, Balkrishna Sharma, Seth Govind Das, H.V. Kamath, Sidhav, Tajamul Husain, Alladi Krishnaswami Ayyar, Naziruddin Ahmad, T.T. Krishnamachari, Loknath Misra. These suggestions were considered by the assembly before finalizing the article.

Right to Freedom (Draft Articles 19–22)

Freedom of Speech etc. (Article 19)

Protection in respect of conviction for offences (Article 20)

Protection of life and personal liberty (Article 21)

Protection against arrest and detention (Article 22)

The sub-committee on Fundamental Rights first considered the rights to freedom of expression, association, assembly etc., as contained in the drafts of Munshi and Ambedkar.

The sub-committee formulated five specific rights of the citizens, viz.,

(i) The right to freedom of speech and expression,

(ii) The right to assemble peacefully and without arms

(iii) The right to form associations or unions

(iv) The right to the secrecy of correspondence

(v) The right to freedom of movement throughout the Union, to reside and settle in any part of the Union, to acquire property, and to follow any occupation, trade, business or profession.

During discussions on this Article various suggestions were made by Alladi Krishnaswami Ayyar, K.T. Shah, Panikkar, Munshi, R.K. Sidhva, Somnath Lahiri, J.J.M. Nichols-Roy, P.S. Deshmukh, Jay Prakash Narayan and Jaipal Singh which were considered by the Assembly. There were more than hundred amendments proposed but almost all were rejected. However, certain amendments moved by Mihir Lal Chatopadhyaya, Munshi and Nichols-Roy were accepted and other amendments were rejected. During the discussion on this article various speakers took active part which included Damodar Swaroop Seth, Mehboob Ali Baig, Hukam Singh, Bhupinder Singh Mann, Syed Karimuddin, Amiyo Kumar Ghosh, Lakshminarayan Sahu, H.J. Khandekar, K.T. Shah, Govind Das, K. Hanumanthaiya, Brajeshwar Prasad, Shibban Lal Saxena, Algu Rai Shastri, Deshbandhu Gupta, T.T. Krishnamachari, Mohamed Ismail, Hasrat Mohani, Jaipal Singh. Further amendments moved by Ambedkar, Chatopadhayay, Munshi and Bhargava were also accepted.

Protection in respect of conviction for offences (Article 20)

The principle of guaranteeing to every person – citizen or alien – protection against *ex post facto* laws, double jeopardy and self-incrimination was provided for in Munshi's draft. Similar provisions were contained in Ambedkar's draft. The provision was non controversial and was adopted by the sub-committee on April 1947.

During discussions various suggestions were made by speakers which included Thakurdas Bhargava, T.T. Krishnamachari, Naziruddin Ahmad, Sayed Karimuddin. The Assembly adopted the amendment moved by Karimuddin, Bhargava and Krishnamachari.

Protection of Life and Personal Liberty (Article 21)

Protection against Arrest and Detention (Article 22)

Munshi's draft, in its chapter on rights to freedom had provided for protection of life and personal liberty. The sub-committee discussed the subject and included two clauses in its draft report. Discussions took place on the subject and various speakers included Alladi Krishanaswami Ayyar, Govind Vallabh Pant, K.M.Pannikar, Sayed Karimuddin, Mehboob Ali Beig, Z.H. Lari, Thakur Das Bhargava, Mrs. Purnima Banerji, H. V. Kamath, P. S. Deshmukh, R. K. Sidhva, Bakshi Tekchand, Jaspat Roy Kapoor, Ananthasayanam Ayyangar, Mahavir Tyagi, Hridayanath Kunjru, Pataskar. Most of the amendments moved were rejected and the amendments moved by Krishnamachari were adopted for article 22.

Right against Exploitation (Articles 23–24)

Prohibition of traffic in human beings and forced labour (Article 23)

Prohibition of employment of children in factories (Article 24)

The right against exploitation was mentioned in the drafts prepared by B.R. Ambedkar, K.M. Munshi and K.T. Shah.

A separate proposal to the effect that military service should be made an exception was rejected by the Assembly. The discussion on the subject was reopened on suggestion by Munshi, and the question of compulsory military service was considered afresh, but the sub-committee again decided to insert a provision prohibiting compulsory military training, as distinguished from military service which was also rejected and instead it was decided to insert a provision similar to the one in the American Constitution against "slavery and involuntary servitude". During discussions on the subject various speakers took active part which included K.T. Shah, Rajkumari Amrit Kaur, Mrs. Hansa Mehta, Alladi Krishnaswami Ayyar, Ambedkar. The Chairman of the committee appointed a small ad hoc committee consisting of Mrs. Hansa Mehta, Rajagopalachari and Govind Ballabh Pant to consider the matter and prepare a suitable draft.

When the two clauses came up for discussion in the Assembly on May 1, 1947, Munshi moved an amendment which was accepted by the Assembly. During discussions various speakers gave suggestions which included Karimuddin, K.T. Shah, Bhupinder Singh Mann, H.V. Kamath, Gurmukh Singh Musafir, Mrs. G. Durgabai, B. Das, Raj Bahadur, T.T. Krishnamachari. All amendments except for K.T. Shah were rejected.

The Assembly rejected all the amendments except the one moved by K.T. Shah.

Right to Freedom of Religion (Draft Articles 25–28)

Freedom of conscience and free profession, practice and propagation of religion (Article 25)

Freedom to manage religious affairs (Article 26)

Freedom as to payment of taxes for promotion of any particular religion (Article 27)

Freedom as to attendance at religious instruction or religious worship in certain educational institutions (Article 28)

The guarantee of religious freedom was contained in the draft articles formulated by Munshi and Ambedkar. The clause in Munshi's draft provided that all citizens would be equally entitled to freedom of conscience and the right freely to profess and practice religion. The right was not unrestricted for it had to be exercised in a manner compatible with public order, morality and health. Economic, financial or political activities associated with religious worship were not to be deemed as being included in the right to profess or practice religion.

The Fundamental Rights sub-committee first discussed freedom of religion and adopted Munshi's clause relating to the right to profess and practice religion with the significant modification that instead of being confined to citizens, the right was extended to all persons. Also, at the instance of Sikh member Harnaam Singh "the right to wear and carry Kirpans" was recognized as part of the practice of the Sikh religion.

Two other clauses – both put forward by B.N. Rau – dealing respectively with the freedom to manage religious affairs, and freedom of attendance at religious instruction in schools, were also adopted. During discussions on these articles various speakers took active part which included Alladi Krishnaswami Ayyar, Rajkumari Amrit Kaur, B.N. Rau, Mrs. Hansa Mehta, Vallabhbhai Patel, Rajagopalachari, Syama Prasad Mukharjee, M. Ruthnaswamy

The committee adopted a compromise by accepting a suggestion made by Rajagopalachari that the clause might be retained but with the qualification that the right of religious denominations to own, acquire and administer property would be subject to the general law. All the clauses were moved in the constituent assembly and few amendments were carried out without controversy. Munshi's amendments were also adopted which sought to ensure that the freedom of religious practice did not come in the way of laws for throwing open Hindu religious institutions of a public character, especially temples, to all classes and sections of Hindus. With regard to the freedom to manage religious affairs various suggestions were given by Mrs. Renuka Ray, Radhakrishna, Kunzru, K.M. Munshi, Vallabhbhai Patel.

After some further debate it was decided to refer the matter to a committee consisting of Mohan Sinha Mehta, Hriday Nath Kunzru, Hussain Imam, S. Radhakrishnan, Mrs. Renuka Ray and K.M. Munshi. This Committee recommended to the drafting committee that a specific provision should be included to the effect that religious instructions should not be permitted in schools run by the state.

When the Draft Constitution was circulated for eliciting opinion, many comments and suggestions were made in regard to the provisions relating to freedom of religion. Of those sent by members, one reiterated the demand for the inclusion of a specific provision prohibiting the recognition of any religion as a State religion and two others aimed at modifying the right conferred by article 19 to "profess and practice" but not to propagate religion. The active participants included Ramalingam Chettiar, Pattabhi Sitaramayya, B.N. Rau, Jaya Prakash Narayan, Mrs. Durgabai, Mohamed Ismail, H.V. Kamath, Lokanath Misra, T.T. Krishnamachari, Tajamul Husain, Ambedkar, Jaspat Roy Kapoor, Abdur Rouf, K.T. Shah, Kamath, Ananthsayanam Ayyangar.

The amendments moved by Ambedkar, Mrs. Durgabai and Kapoor, were accepted and the draft article adopted.

Cultural and Educational Rights (Articles 29-30)

Protection of interests of minorities (Article 29)

Right of Minorities to establish and administer educational institutions (Article 30)

A guarantee of the protection of the cultural and educational rights of linguistic and religious minorities was contained in the drafts prepared by K.M. Munshi, K.T. Shah and Harnam Singh. Many members took active part in the discussions which included Munshi, Govind Ballabh Pant, Sardar Ujjal Singh, Mohanlal Saxena, Mahavir Tyagi, Hussain Imam, Hriday Nath Kunzru, Mrs. Purnima Banerji, B.N.Rau, Pattabhi Sitaramayya, R.R. Diwakar, S.V. Krishnamoorthy Rao, Jaya Prakash Narayan.

The Drafting committee accepted two amendments; one, suggested by itself, replacing the words "language, script and culture" by the words "language, script or culture" and the other, suggested by Diwakar, Krishnamoorthy Rao, and Mrs. Purnima Banerji, seeking to provide that State-aided educational institutions (as well as State-owned institutions) should not discriminate against any minority in the matter of admission. This draft article came up before the constituent assembly for consideration and out of the original 43 amendments only about a dozen were actually moved. The amendments moved by Ambedkar and Thakur Das Bhargava were accepted. Amendments were also moved by Lokanath Misra, Damodar Swarup Seth, Jaya Prakash Narayan, K.T. Shah, Z.H. Lahiri, Karimuddin, Begum Aizaz Rasul, M.l. Chattopadhyay, R.K. Sidhva, Jaipal Singh, Santhanam, Govind Ballabh Pant, H.N. Kunzru, but these were rejected.

Right to Property (Article 31)

Compulsory acquisition of property (Article 31)

The original draft article dealing with the "Right to property " was prepared by Munshi, the explanatory notes were given by B.N. Rau, who also suggested the insertion of a new clause declaring that the state may limit the rights guaranteed in relation to the property whenever the exigencies of the common good so required. During discussions various speakers gave their views which included K.T. Shah, Munshi, Rajkumari Amrit Kaur, Mrs. Hansa Mehta, B.N. Rau, Govind Ballabh Pant, Alladi Krishnaswami Ayyar, Panikkar, A.P. Jain, V.D. Tripathi,

R.K. Sidhva, V.C. Kesava Rao, Phool Singh, Syamanandan Sahaya, Jay Prakash Narayan, Guptanath Singh, T.T. Krishnamachari, Damodar Swarup Seth, Shibban Lal Saxena, H.V. Kamath, Mrs. Renuka Ray, Thakurdas Bhargava, Mahboob Ali Baig, B. Das, Ahmed Ibrahim, Naziruddin Ahmed, Jaspat Roy Kapoor, Kala Venkata Rao, K.M. Munshi,

Munshi supported the amendments moved by Kapoor. Regarding laws relating to evacuee property, Kala Venkata Rao's amendment for the replacement of words "one year" by the words "18 months" was accepted. The article as amended was finally accepted by the constituent assembly.

Right to Constitutional Remedies (Article 32-35)

Remedies for enforcement of Fundamental Rights (Article 32)

Power to Parliament to modify fundamental rights in their application to Armed Forces (Article 33)

Restriction on fundamental rights while martial law is in force in any area (Article 34)

Legislation to give effect to fundamental rights (Article 35)

The idea of providing in the Constitution effective remedies for the enforcement of the fundamental rights was from the very beginning present in the minds of its framers. When the sub-committee on Fundamental Rights assembled first on February 27, 1947, Alladi Krishnaswamy Ayyar pointed out that the citizen's rights to be embodied in the Constitution should consist of guarantees enforceable in courts of law.

In his note on fundamental rights Munshi also stressed the need for the same. Accordingly, in Munshi's draft provisions on fundamental rights, the right to constitutional remedies was incorporated as a fundamental right: courts within the Union could be moved for the issue of four writs of right, namely, (a) the writ of person (*habeas corpus*) to secure the release of any one from unlawful or unjustifiable deprivation of the right of personal liberty, (b) the writ of enforcement (*mandamus*) to secure the performance of any specific act by a unit, an officer or a corporation in the discharge of a definite public duty, obligation or requirement with which it was specifically charged by the Constitution or by any law, (c) the writ of prohibition, prohibiting any court (other than the Supreme Court) or tribunal from continuing proceedings in contravention of the Constitution or in excess of jurisdiction vested in or by law, and (d) the writ of direction (*certiorari*) for directing a judge (other than a judge of the Supreme Court) or a person or body vested with judicial functions to transmit the record of proceedings pending before him or it and involving a question of a right or a duty for the purpose of quashing the proceedings or referring them to the appropriate tribunal. These writs, however, could not be invoked during the existence of a state of war, armed rebellion or a grave emergency.

Ambedkar's draft article differed from Munshi's proposals in that it vested the authority to issue prerogative writs exclusively in the Supreme Court and included an additional writ – the writ of *quo warranto*. Ambedkar was also strongly in favour of the power of prerogative writs as a speedy and effective means of guaranteeing fundamental rights. During discussion, various speakers gave suggestions and moved amendments which included Alladi Krishnaswami Ayyar, Munshi, Ambedkar, K. Santhanam, Vallabhbhai Patel, B.N. Rau, R.K. Sidhva, Tajamul Husain, Naziruddin Ahmad, Kamath, Karimuddin, N.G. Ranga, Shibban Lal Saxena, Rohini Kumar Choudhary, Sarwate,

The amendments moved by Ambedkar and Naziruddin Ahmad were adopted by the Assembly and all others negatived.

With regard to Power of Parliament to modify fundamental rights in their application to Armed Forces (Article 33) and Restriction on fundamental rights while martial law is in force in any area (Article 34), no amendments of substance were moved and it was adopted by the Assembly with a minor verbal change suggested by Ambedkar.

When the changes made by the Drafting Committee at the revision stage were considered by the Constituent Assembly on November 14, 1949, a number of amendments and suggestions to the new article 34 were proposed by members which included Shibban Lal Saxena, Kamath and Ambedkar. The amendments of Saxena and Kamath were negatived by the Assembly and the new Article 34 was adopted in the form in which it was proposed by Drafting Committee.

With regard to Legislation to give effect to fundamental rights (article 35) discussions took place and some suggestions and amendments were moved by speakers which included K.M. Panikkar, H.V. Kamath and Ambedkar. This draft article came up before the constituent assembly for consideration on December 9, 1948, and there was hardly any discussion and no further amendments were proposed and the draft article was adopted as such.

Final Shape of Articles on Fundamental Rights

The original draft articles as submitted by the drafting committee consisted of the articles 14-35 as stated above. However, after adoption of the articles on fundamental rights, when the final shape of the Constitution took place, the fundamental rights were incorporated in part III of the Constitution and as articles 12-35. (Shown at Annexure-1). The articles on fundamental rights were subsequently amended but the said amendments and persons responsible/taking part in the discussions for the same are not being covered herein.

Annexure 1

Part III

FUNDAMENTAL RIGHTS

Article No.	Nomenclature
12	Definition
13	Laws inconsistent with or in derogation of the fundamental rights
14	Equality before Law
15	Prohibition of discrimination on grounds of religion, race, caste, sex or place of birth
16	Equality of opportunity in matters of public employment
17	Abolition of Untouchability
18	Abolition of titles
19	Protection of certain rights regarding freedom of speech, etc.
20	Protection in respect of conviction for offences
21	Protection of life and personal liberty
22	Protection against arrest and detention in certain cases
23	Prohibition of traffic in human beings and forced labour
24	Prohibition of employment of children in factories, etc.
25	Freedom of conscience and free profession, practice and propagation of religion
26	Freedom to manage religious affairs
27	Freedom as to payment of taxes for promotion of any particular religion
28	Freedom as to attendance at religious instruction or religious worship in certain educational institutions
29	Protection of interests of minorities
30	Right of minorities to establish and administer educational institutions
31	Compulsory acquisition of property
32	Remedies for enforcement of rights conferred by this part
33	Power of Parliament to modify the rights conferred by this part in their application to Forces, etc.
34	Restriction on rights conferred by this part while martial law is in force in any area
35	Legislation to give effect to the provisions of this part

Chapter XIV
Adoption of the Constitution – November 26, 1949

The Constituent Assembly took up the third reading of the Constitution on November 17, 1949, on a motion by Dr. B.R. Ambedkar "that the Constitution as settled by the Assembly be passed". The discussion on the motion concluded on November 26 and the motion was put to vote and adopted amidst prolonged cheers.

DR. B.R. AMBEDKAR'S SPEECH—NOVEMBER 25, 1949

Dr. B.R. Ambedkar pointed out that looking back on the work of the Constituent Assembly it will now be two years, eleven months and seventeen days since it first met on 9th December, 1946. Dr. B.R. Ambedkar then pointed out to the work done in the past 11 sessions. Dr. Ambedkar thereafter referred to the drafting Committee which was elected by the Constituent Assembly on 29th August, 1947 and referred to drafting Committee's drafts and noted the fact that the total number of amendments of the draft Constitution tabled in the House was approximately 7635 and the total number of amendments actually moved in the House were 2473. Dr. Ambedkar compared the time consumed by the Constituent Assembly in various countries like American Convention, Constitutional Convention of Canada, Australian Constitutional Convention and the South African Convention.

Dr. Ambedkar pointed out that the American Convention completed its work within four months and the Constitutional Convention of Canada took a period of 2 years and five months and the Australian Constitutional Convention consumed a period of 9 years and the South African Convention spent one year's labour in completing the Constitution.

Dr. Ambedkar pointed out that the Constitution of America, Canada, South Africa and Australia are much smaller than our Constitution and further stated that the makers of the Constitution of America, Canada, Australia and South Africa did not have to face the problem of amendments.

Dr. Ambedkar pointed out that except for a solitary member *viz.* Mr. Naziruddin Ahmed; there was a general consensus of appreciation from all members of the Constituent Assembly to the work done by the Drafting Committee.

Dr. B.R. Ambedkar pointed out the condemnation of the Constitution largely came from two quarters, the Communist party and the Socialist party in the following manner:—

> "Why do they condemn the Constitution? Is it because it is really a bad Constitution? I venture to say 'no'. The Communist party wants a Constitution based upon the principle of the Dictatorship of the Proletariat. They condemn the Constitution because it is based upon Parliamentary democracy."

Dr. B.R. Ambedkar referred to the statement of Jefferson, the great American statesman in the following manner:—

> "We may consider each generation as a distinct nation, with a right, by the will of the majority, to bind themselves, but none to bind the succeeding generation, more than the inhabitants of another country. The idea that institutions established for the use of the nation cannot be touched or modified, even to make them answer their end, because of

rights gratuitously supposed in those employed to manage them in the trust for the public, may perhaps be a salutary provision against the abuses of a monarch, but is most absurd against the nation itself. Yet our lawyers and priests generally inculcate this doctrine, and suppose that preceding generations held the earth more freely than we do; had a right to impose laws on us, unalterable by ourselves, and that we, in the like manner, can make laws and impose burdens on future generations, which they will have no right to alter; in fine, that the earth belongs to the dead and not the living."

Regarding the power to amend this is what Dr. Amedkar said in the following manner:—

"The Assembly has not only refrained from putting a seal of finality and infallibility upon this Constitution by denying to the people the right to amend the Constitution as in Canada or by making the amendment of the Constitution subject to the fulfillment of extraordinary terms and conditions as in America or Australia, but has provided a most facile procedure for amending the Constitution. I challenge any of the critics of the Constitution to prove that any Constituent Assembly anywhere in the world has, in the circumstances in which this country finds itself, provided such a facile procedure for the amendment of the Constitution. If those who are dissatisfied with the Constitution have only to obtain a two-thirds majority and if they cannot obtain even a two-thirds majority in the Parliament elected on adult franchise in their favour, their dissatisfaction with the Constitution cannot be deemed to be shared by the general public.

Regarding the objection that the Constitution can be called centralism, this is what he said in the following manner:—

> "The States under our Constitution are in no way dependent upon the Centre for their legislative or executive authority. The Centre and the States are co-equal in this matter. It is difficult to see how such a Constitution can be called centralism."

Regarding the powers of the Centre and the judiciary to alter the boundaries of the partition, this is what he said in the following manner:—

> "Courts may modify, they cannot replace. They can revise earlier interpretations as new arguments, new points of view are presented, they can shift the dividing line in marginal cases, but there are barriers they cannot pass, definite assignments of power they cannot reallocate. They can give a broadening construction of existing powers, but they cannot assign to one authority powers explicitly granted to another.

The second charge is that the Centre has been given the power to override the States. This charge must be admitted. But before condemning the Constitution for containing such overriding powers, certain considerations must be borne in mind. The first is that these overriding powers do not form the normal feature of the Constitution. Their use and operation are expressly confined to emergencies only. The second consideration: Could we avoid giving overriding powers to the Centre when an emergency has arisen?"

Regarding the powers to the Centre in case of emergency, this is what he has said in the following manner:—

> "There can be no doubt that in the opinion of the vast majority of the people, the residual loyalty of the citizen in an emergency must be to the Centre and not to the constituent States. For it is only the Centre which can work for a common end and for

the general interests of the country as a whole. Herein lays the justification for giving to the Centre certain overriding powers to be used in an emergency. And after all what is the obligation imposed upon the constituent States by these emergency powers? No more than this – that in an emergency, they should take into consideration alongside their own local interests, the opinions and interests of the nation as a whole. Only those who have not understood the problem, can complain against it."

Dr. B.R. Ambedkar referred to the future of this country in the following manner:—

"On 26th January, 1950, India will be an independent country (cheers). What would happen to her independence? Will she maintain her independence or will she lose it again? This is the first thought that comes to my mind. It is not that India was never an independent country. The point is that she once lost the independence she had. Will she lose it a second time? Will history repeat itself? It is this thought which fills me with anxiety. This eventuality we must all resolutely guard against. We must be determined to defend our independence with the last drop of our blood (cheers)."

Dr. B.R. Ambedkar further pointed out that it is not that India did not know Parliament or Parliament procedure. He further pointed out that we wish to maintain democracy; we have to abandon the bloody methods of revolution in the following manner:—

"The first thing in my judgment we must do is to hold fast to constitutional methods of achieving our social and economic objectives. It means we must abandon the bloody methods of revolution."

He further pointed out that—

"The second thing we must do is to observe the caution which John Stuart Mill has given to all who are interested in the maintenance of democracy, namely, not to lay their liberties at the feet of even a great man, or to trust him with powers which enable him to subvert their institutions". There is nothing wrong in being grateful to great men who have rendered life-long services to the country. But there are limits to gratefulness. As has been said by the Irish patriot Daniel O'Connell, no man can be grateful at the cost of his honour, no woman can be grateful at the cost of her chastity and no nation can be grateful at the cost of its liberty. This caution is far more necessary in the case of India than in the case of any other country. For in India, *Bhakti* or what may be called the path of devotion or hero-worship, plays a part in its politics unequalled in magnitude by the part it plays in the politics of any other country in the world. *Bhakti* in religion may be a road to the salvation of the soul. But in politics, *Bhakti* or hero-worship is a sure road to degradation and to eventual dictatorship.

The third thing we must do is not to be content with mere political democracy. We must make our political democracy a social democracy as well. Political democracy cannot last unless there lies at the base of it social democracy. What does social democracy mean? It means a way of life which recognizes liberty, equality and fraternity as the principles of life. These principles of liberty, equality and fraternity are not to be treated as separate items in a trinity. They form a union of trinity in the sense that to divorce one from the other is to defeat the very purpose of democracy.

> We must begin by acknowledging the fact that there is complete absence of two things in Indian society. One of these is equality. On the social plane, we have in India a society based on the principle of graded inequality which means elevation for some and degradation for others. On the economic plane, we have a society in which there are some who have immense wealth as against many who live in abject poverty."

On caste system, Dr. B.R. Ambedkar said that "in India there are castes. These castes are anti-national, in the first place because they generate jealousy and antipathy between caste and caste. But we must overcome all these difficulties if we wish to become a nation in reality. For fraternity can be a fact only when there is a nation. Without fraternity, equality and liberty will be no deeper than coats of paints."

Dr. B.R. Ambedkar quoted from what has been said by Abraham Lincoln that House divided against itself cannot stand very long in the following manner:—

> "They are prepared to have Government for the people and are indifferent whether it is Government of the people and by the people. If we wish to preserve the Constitution in which we have sought to enshrine the principle of Government of the people, for the people and by the people, let us resolve not to be tardy in the recognition of the evils that lie across our path and which induce people to prefer Government for the people to Government by the people, nor to be weak in our initiative to remove them. That is the only way to serve the country. I know of no better."

It is remarkable that the entire speech of Dr. B.R. Ambedkar stands out as a great reminder to the people about the importance of following the constitutional methods in achieving rightful place for this country in the comity of nations, also shows his great learning and knowledge of the Constitutional law of the various countries of the world.

The Framing of India's Constitution – Select Documents (Vol. 4) by B. Shiva Rao, pages 935 to 946.

Chapter XV

Speech of Dr. Rajendra Prasad – November 26, 1949 and Final Adoption of the Constitution

Dr. Rajendra Prasad in his opening speech desired to congratulate the Assembly on accomplishing a task of such tremendous magnitude. He further pointed out in the beginning. "Some facts which will show the tremendousness of the task which we undertook some three years back. Here, in spite of the size of the population and the country, we have succeeded in framing a Constitution which covers the whole of it. Apart from the size, there were other difficulties which were inherent in the problem itself. We have got many communities living in this country. We have got many languages prevalent in different parts of it. We have got other kinds of differences dividing the people in the different parts from one another. We had to make provision not only for areas which are advanced educationally and economically: we had also to make provision for backward people like the Tribes and for backward areas like the Tribal Areas. The communal problem had been one of the knottiest problems which the country has had before it for a pretty long time."

Dr. Rajendra Prasad then pointed out to another problem of great magnitude which was the problem of the Indian States. When the British came to India, they did not conquer the country as a whole or at one stroke. They got bits of it from time-to-time.

Dr. Rajendra Prasad further pointed out:—

"The paramountcy which they had so long exercised and by which they could keep the Princes in order also lapsed. The Indian Government was then faced with the problem of tackling these States which had different traditions of rule, some of them having some form of popular representation in Assemblies and some having no resemblance in anything like that, and governing completely autocratically.

In course of time not only have all the smaller States coalesced and become integrated with some Province or other of India but some of the larger ones also have joined. Many of the States have formed Unions of their own and such Unions have become part of the Indian Union. It must be said to the credit of the Princes and the people of the States no less than to the credit of the States Ministry under the wise and far-sighted guidance of Sardar Vallabhbhai Patel that by the time we have been able to pass this Constitution, the States are now more or less in the same position as the Provinces and it has become possible to describe all of them including the Indian States and the Provinces as States in the Constitution. The announcement which has been made just now by Sardar Vallabhbhai Patel makes the position very clear, and now there is no difference between the States, as understood before, and the Provinces in the new Constitution."

Dr. Rajendra Prasad then pointed out that cost too which the Assembly has had to incur during its three years' existence is not too high when you take into consideration the factors going to constitute it. I understand that the expenses up to the 22nd of November come to Rs. 63,96,729.

The method which the Constituent Assembly adopted in connection with the Constitution was first to lay down its terms of reference as it were in the form of an Objectives Resolution which was moved by Pandit Jawaharlal Nehru in an inspiring speech and which constitutes now the Preamble to our Constitution."

Dr. Rajendra Prasad thereafter referred to the various committees formed to deal with different aspects of the constitutional problem. He further referred to the role played by Pt. Jawaharlal Nehru and Sardar Patel, who presided over various committees. He also paid tributes to Mr. B.N. Rau, who brought to bear on his task a detailed knowledge of constitutions of other countries and extensive knowledge of the conditions of this country as well as his own administrative experience.

Dr. Rajendra Prasad thereafter referred to the silent features of the Constitution. He further pointed out that "the first and the most obvious fact which will attract any observer is the fact that we are going to have a Republic. India knew republics in the past olden days, but that was 2,000 years ago or more and those republics were small republics. We never had anything like the Republic which we are going to have now, although there were empires in those days as well as during the Mughal period which covered very large parts of the country. The President of the Republic will be an elected President. We never have had an elected Head of the State which covered such a large area of India. It thus comes about that, while the Parliament and Legislative Assemblies are elected by the adult population of the country as a whole, the President is elected by representatives who represent the entire population twice over, once as representatives of the states and again as their representatives in the Central Parliament of the country. But although the President is elected by the same electorate as the Central and Sate

Legislature, it is as well that his position is that of a Constitutional President."

Dr. Rajendra Prasad thereafter referred to the role of the Ministers in the present Constitution. He also referred to the role of the two Houses known as the House of the People and the Council of States which both together constitute the Parliament of India. He thereafter referred to the election of the Legislative Assemblies and the House of the People by adult suffrage.

Dr. Rajendra Prasad forcefully advocated the case of providing for adult franchise in the following fashion:—

> "In my opinion, our people possess intelligence and common sense. They also have a culture which the sophisticated people of today may not appreciate, but which is solid. They are not literate and do not possess the mechanical skill of reading and writing. But, I have no doubt in my mind that they are able to take measure of their own interest and also of the interests of the country at large if things are explained to them".

Dr. Rajendra Prasad thereafter referred to the role to be played by the second chamber. Regarding the role of the judiciary this is what he said:—

> "We have provided in the Constitution for a judiciary which will be independent. It is difficult to suggest anything more to make the Supreme Court and the High Courts independent of the influence of the executive."

He also referred to the independent agencies like Public Service Commission, Comptroller and Auditor-General and the Election Commission. Regarding distribution of powers and functions between the Union and the States this is what he said—

> "The Constitution has gone into great details regarding the distribution of power and functions

> between the Union and the States in all aspects of their administrative and other activities. It has been said by some that the powers given to the Centre are too many and too extensive and the States have been deprived of power which should really belong to them in their own fields.

Powers have been very meticulously and elaborately defined and demarcated in the three lists of the Seventh Schedule, and the residue, whatever it may be, is not likely to cover any large field, and, therefore, the vesting of such residuary powers does not mean any very serious derogation in fact from the power which ought to belong to the States."

Regarding the official language this is what he said—

> "The use of English during the period of transition was considered inevitable for practical reasons and no one need be despondent over this decision, which has been dictated purely by practical considerations. It is the duty of the country as a whole now and especially of those whose language is Hindi to so shape and develop it as to make it the language in which the composite culture of India can find its expression adequately and nobly."

Regarding the Directive Principles this is what he said—

> "In a world torn with conflicts, in a world which even after the devastation of two world wars is still depending on armaments to establish peace and goodwill, we are destined to play a great part, if we prove true to the teachings of the Father of the Nation and give effect to this Directive Principle in our Constitution."

Regarding the qualifications necessary for the Members of the Legislatures, he pointed two regrets—

> "I would have liked to have some qualifications laid down for members of the Legislatures. It is anomalous that we should insist upon high qualifications for those who administer or help in administering the law but none for those who make it except that they are elected. A law giver requires intellectual equipment but even more than that capacity to take a balanced view of things, to act independently and above all to be true to those fundamental things of life – in one world, to have character."

The other regret is that we have not been able to draw up our first Constitution of a free Bharat in an Indian language. The difficulties in both cases were practical and proved insurmountable. But that does not make the regret any the less poignant".

He further pointed out to the role of the administrators in the following manner:—

> "Whatever the Constitution may or may not provide, the welfare of the country will depend upon the way in which the country is administered. That will depend upon the men who administer it. After all, a Constitution like a machine is a lifeless thing. It acquires life because of the men who control it and operate it, and India needs today nothing more than a set of honest men who will have the interest of the country before them. It requires men of strong character, men of vision, men who will not sacrifice the interests of the country at large for the sake of smaller groups and areas and who will rise over the prejudices which are born of these differences."

In the end he paid compliments to the Constitutional Adviser Shri B.N. Rau, Shri S.N. Mukherjee, who had proved of such invaluable help to the Drafting Committee,

Secretary Mr. H.V.R. Iengar, who organized the Secretariat amongst others.

At the end the Resolution moved by Dr. B.R. Ambedkar and as settled by the Assembly was passed amongst prolonged cheers.

Thus ended the Saga of the Final Adoption of the Constitution.

The Framing of India's Constitution – Select Documents (Vol. 4) by B. Shiva Rao, pages 946 to 960.

PART III

BIOGRAPHIES OF FAMOUS FRAMERS OF THE INDIAN CONSTITUTION

DR. RAJENDRA PRASAD

(December 3, 1884 – February 28, 1963)

"Dr. Rajendra Prasad played an important role in formation and functioning of the Constituent Assembly. Dr. Rajendra Prasad was elected as the President of the Constituent Assembly. Dr. Rajendra Prasad was the Chairman of the Steering Committee, Chairman on the Committee on the Rules of Procedure, Chairman of Finance and Staff Committee, Chairman of *Ad-hoc* Committee on the National Flag. The Constitution of India was promulgated on November 26, 1949 and was adopted and ratified by the Constituent Assembly on 26th January, 1950. Dr. Rajendra Prasad was elected the first President of India".

Dr. Rajendra Prasad was the first President of the Republic of India. He was an independence activist and, as a leader of the Congress Party, he played a prominent role in the Indian Indepedence Movement. He served as President of the Constituent Assembly that drafted the Consitution of the Republic from 1948 to 1950. He had also served as a Cabinet Minister briefly in the first Government of Independent India.

Dr. Rajendra Prasad, son of Mahadev Sahai, was born in Zeradei village in Bihar on December 3, 1884. Being the youngest in a large joint family "Rajen" was greatly loved and was strongly attached to his mother and elder brother Mahendra.

Dr. Rajendra Prasad was a brilliant student throughout school and college. He stood first in the entrance examination of the University of Calcutta and was awarded a Rs. 30 per month scholarship. It was for the first time that a student from Bihar had excelled. He joined the Calcutta Presidency College in 1902.

In 1915, Rajen passed the Masters Degree in Law examination with honours, winning a gold medal. He then completed his Doctorate in Law to attain the title, Dr. Rajendra Prasad.

While Gandhiji was on a fact-finding mission in Chamaparan district of Bihar, he called on Rajendra Prasad to come to Champaran with volunteers. Dr. Prasad rushed to Champaran. Dr. Prasad was deeply moved by the dedication, conviction and courage that Gandhiji displayed. Here was a man alien to the parts, who had made the cause of the people of Champaran his cause. Dr. Prasad became Gandhiji's dedicated follower, thereafter. Gandhiji's influence greatly altered many of Dr. Prasad's views, most importantly, on untouchability.

Whenever the people suffered, Dr. Prasad was present to help reduce the pain. In 1914 floods ravaged Bihar and Bengal. Dr. Prasad became a volunteer distributing food and clothes to the flood victims. In 1934, Bihar was shaken by an earthquake. The quake caused immense damage and loss of property. He did not rest. He set up relief committees in Sind and Punjab for the homeless victims that flocked there.

Dr. Prasad was shocked by the Government atrocities at Jallianwalla Bagh. He called for non-cooperation in Bihar as part of Gandhiji's non-cooperation movement. Dr. Prasad gave up his law practice and started a National College near Patna in 1921. The college was later shifted to Sadaqat Ashram on the banks of the Ganga. In connection with the non-cooperation movement which spread like wildfire in Bihar, Dr. Prasad toured the State, holding public meetings one after another, collecting funds and galvanizing the nation for a complete boycott of all schools, colleges and Government offices. He urged the people to take to spinning and wear only khadi. Bihar and the entire nation was taken by storm; the people responded to the leaders' call.

In March 1930, Gandhiji launched the Salt Satyagraha. He planned to march from Sabarmati Ashram to Dandi seashore to break the salt laws. A Salt Satyagraha was launched in Bihar under Dr. Prasad. Nakhas Pond in Patna was chosen as the site of the *satyagraha*. Batch after batch of volunteers courted arrest while making salt. Many volunteers were injured. Dr. Prasad called for more volunteers. Public opinion forced the Government to retract the police and allow the volunteers to make salt. Dr. Rajendra Prasad played an important role in the movement and he was sentenced to six months' imprisonment.

Dr. Prasad presided over the Bombay session of the Indian National Congress in October 1934. Following the resignation of Subhash Chandra Bose as the President of the Congress in April 1939, Dr. Prasad was elected President. He did his best to heal the rifts created between the incompatible ideology of Subhash Chandra Bose and Gandhiji.

As the freedom struggle progressed, the dark shadow of communalism which had always lurked in the background, steadily grew to engulf the country. To Dr. Prasad's dismay communal riots began to burst spontaneously all over the nation and in Bihar. He rushed from one scene to another to control the riots.

A Constituent Assembly was formed in July 1946, to frame the Constitution of India and Dr. Rajendra Prasad was elected its President. On November 26, 1946 the

Constitution of India was adopted by the constituent Assembly. On January 26, 1950, the Constitution was ratified and Dr. Rajendra Prasad was elected the first President of India. Dr. Prasad transformed the regal splendour of Rashtrapati Bhavan into an elegant "Indian" home. Dr. Prasad visited many countries on missions of goodwill. He stressed for peace in a nuclear age. He was awarded the highest civilian award of India, the **'Bharat Ratna'.** Dr. Prasad authored many books including his autobiography "Atmakatha" (1946), "Satyagraha at Champaran" (1922), "India Divided" (1946), "Mahatma Gandhi and Bihar, Some Reminiscences" (1949), and "Bapu Ke Kadmon Mein" (1954).

He was the first President who on his retirement passed in a horse-riden carriage throughout the streets of Delhi acknowledging high respect and acclamation of the people of the capital of India.

Dr. Prasad spent the last few months of his life at the Sadaqat Ashram in Patna. He died on February 28, 1963.[1]

---

1. Dr. Rajendra Prasad Biography taken from Internet.

Soli J Sorabjee, Pradeep Arora, Keshav Dayal, Justice P Sathasivam, Dr Manish Arora and Justice Madan B Lokur at release of first edition of the book "Makers of Indian Constitution".

Justice P Sathasivam addressing the gathering at Book release function.

O.P. Faizi, Prof M P Singh, Justice Madan B Lokur, Soli J Sorabjee, Keshav Dayal, Justice P Sathasivam and Deepak Dayal at the Book Release venue.

Deepak Dayal addressing at the book release function. Others on the Dias: Dr Manish Arora, Soli J Sorabjee, Justice P Sathasivam, Justice Madan B Lokur and Keshav Dayal

Keshav Dayal Presenting the books to Hon'ble Lt Governor of Delhi.

Author Keshav Dayal being honoured at the Book Club Event 2013 at Delhi Gymkhana Club on 31st May, 2013.

Author Keshav Dayal giving a talk on his book at Delhi Gymkhana Club on 31st May, 2013.

Audience at Delhi Gymkhana Club event.

PANDIT JAWAHARLAL NEHRU

(14 November, 1889 – 27 May, 1964)

"Pandit Jawaharlal Nehru was the first Prime Minister of India. Pandit Jawaharlal Nehru was the Chairman of the Experts Committee, Union Power Committee, Union Constitution Committee and member of States Committee.

Pandit Jawaharlal Nehru moved a historic resolution on December 13, 1946 after four days of the first session of the Constituent Assembly outlining the main objectives of the Constitution. Pandit Jawaharlal Nehru made a memorable speech placing the historic objectives of the Constitution."

Pandit Jawaharlal Nehru was an Indian statesman who was the first, and the longest-serving Prime Minister of India so far, having served from 1947 to 1964. A leading figure in the Indian independence movement, Nehru was elected by the Congress Party to assume office as independent India's first Prime Minister, and later when the Congress won India's first general election in 1952. As one of the founders of the Non-aligned Movement, he was also an important figure in the international politics of the post-war era.

Pandit Jawaharlal Nehru has been aptly described as idol of the Indian masses, successor to Mahatma Gandhi, Champion of the Oppressed and symbol of new India.[1]

1. Michael Brecher—A Political Biography of Nehru, p. 5, published by Oxford University Press.

Jawaharlal Nehru was born on 14th November, 1889 in the city of Allahabad, situated along the banks of the Ganges River (now in the State of Uttar Pradesh). *Jawahar* means a "gem" in Arabic and is a name similar in meaning to *moti,* "pearl". He was the eldest child of the eminent and well-known Barrister, Motilal Nehru. From his father Jawaharlal inherited or acquired certain qualities which remain embedded in his personality. Among these was pride in his own achievements, in his family, in his Kashmiri ancestry and in his people.[1] After being tutored at home and attending some of the most modern schools in India, Nehru travelled to England at the age of 15 to attend Harrow. He proceeded to study natural sciences at Trinity College, Cambridge before choosing to get training as Barrister at the Inner Temple in London, frequenting the theatres, museums and Opera Houses of London. He was called to the Bar in 1912. With his education completed, he returned to India after seven formative years in the country against which he was to struggle much of his adult life, and at whose hands he was to undergo imprisonment for nine years.[2]

Upon his return to India, Nehru's marriage was arranged with Kamala Kaul. At the time of marriage on February 8, 1916 Nehru's age was 27 and his bride was 16 years old. Their only child Indira Priyadarshani better known as Mrs. Indira Gandhi was born on 19th November, 1917. He joined Congress under the patronage of his father. His father was a prominent figure in the Congress deliberations at the time, as he was to remain until his death in 1931. Throughout that period Jawaharlal was overshadowed by his father, among others, certainly until

---

1. Michael Brecher: A Political Biography of Nehru, p. 41, published by Oxford University Press.
2. Michael Brecher: A Political Biography of Nehru, p. 51, published by Oxford University Press.

1929, when he succeeded him as Congress President.[1] Although frequently hailed as a future leader of the Congress and India, Nehru's political rise did not begin until the arrival of Mahatma Gandhi on India's political arena. Their first meeting took place at the end of 1916. Nehru's impression of Gandhiji, as recorded in, 'Towards Freedom', "All of us admired him for his heroic fight in South Africa, but he seemed very distant and different and unpolitical to many of us young men[2]." What brought them together was a fortuitous set of circumstances.

The Montagu-Chelmsford Report on Constitutional reforms was published in June, 1918. A special session of the Congress was held in Bombay to consider the proposals, which were far short of the expectations, and the Congress demanded 'self-government within the Empire'. The necessary shock was provided early in 1919 by the Rowlatt Bills and the Amritsar Tragedy; To galvanise mass support for this act of defiance Gandhiji proclaimed 6 April as *Satyagraha* Day, a day of hartal (suspension of all business), a day of fasting, a day of mass meetings to protest against the hated legislation. There were a few incidents of violence, but Martial law was proclaimed, and public meetings were banned. Despite the ban on public meetings, the Congress organized a mammoth meeting on 13 April, the Hindu New Year Day. An estimated 20,000 people gathered in the Jallianwalla Bagh. Suddenly there appeared at the entrance 150 soldiers under the command of General Dyer. The crowd was ordered to disperse, but there was no way out; the military blocked the only exit. Within three minutes, an order was given to fire at point-blank range on the unarmed masses. According to the Hunter

1. Michael Brecher: A Political Biography of Nehru, p. 55, published by Oxford University Press.
2. Michael Brecher: A Political Biography of Nehru, p. 60, published by Oxford University Press.

Commission of Inquiry, 379 were killed and about 1,200 were wounded. The only reason the others were spared, according to Dyer's own testimony before the Commission was that he had exhausted his ammunition. Jallianwalla Bagh became hallowed ground and the shooting a day of rememberance for the Congress.

The Punjab tragedy roused Indians as no other act since the Rebellion of 1857. For Nehru, along with many others, it was a profound insult to the national honour, pride and self-respect. The Amritsar Tragedy in particular was for him the first great shock as an Indian, and as such it provoked an instinctive response. The slaughter at Jallianwalla Bagh was the darkest day in Nehru's life.

The Nagpur session proved to be a landmark in many respects. Gandhi's undisputed leadership was acknowledged for the first time. Moreover, the Congress' goal was officially changed to 'the attainment of *Swaraj*.... By all legitimate and peaceful means, a radical departure from the previous goal of self-government within the Empire'. Gandhiji inspired his countrymen as early as 1922. The Mahatma's personal influence at that time, on Jawaharlal Nehru was remarkable, and Mahatma's spell was all embracing.

Following Gandhiji's example, Nehru and his family abandoned their Western-style clothes, possessions and wealthy lifestyle. Wearing clothes spun out of *khadi*, Nehru emerged as one of the most energetic supporters of Gandhi. Under Gandhiji's influence, Nehru began studying the *Bhagavad Gita* and practised yoga throughout his life. He increasingly looked to Gandhiji for advice and guidance in his personal life, and spent a lot of time travelling and living with Gandhiji.

To court imprisonment deliberately and openly was the supreme obligation of those who followed the creed of *Satyagraha*. To be sent to jail was a mark of distinction and success. But the reality of life in prison was completely unknown to Nehru in 1921. It was shrouded in mystery and associated with social degradation and isolation. With the passage of time jail became a second home, for he returned nine times, some of them for short terms. Altogether, he spent about nine years away from family, home, friends and work.

Above all, it was a phase of mental and emotional growth. The young Brahmin had become eager and devoted political worker, fired by the goal of Indian freedom and the example of Gandhiji. For this was the period in which he discovered the Mahatma and came under his influence, a relationship which profoundly shaped his future as a man and a statesman. He had also discovered the peasants and had seen their miserable conditions of life. He had overcome his aversion to public speaking and had established the basis of communion with the masses, from which he later derived spiritual strength and political power. India attained freedom on the historic date 15th of August, 1947. On the eve of independence, Pandit Nehru addressed the Constituent Assembly, in the following historic words:—

> "We made a tryst with destiny, and now the time comes when we shall redeem our pledge, not wholly or in full measure, but very substantially. At the stroke of the midnight hour, when the world sleeps, India will awake to life and freedom. A moment comes, which comes but rarely in history, when we step out from the old to the new, when an age ends, and when the soul of a nation, long suppressed, finds utterance. It is fitting that at this solemn moment we take the pledge of dedication to the service of India and her people and to the still higher course of humanity[1]." (355-356)

1. Michael Brecher: A Political Biography of Nehru, pp. 355-356, published by Oxford University Press.

On the Independence Day 15th August, 1947 the celebrations were brought to a close with an impressive flag-hoisting ceremony at the Red Fort which was the majestic symbol of Moghul power and splendour in Old Delhi. A crowd estimated at half a million gathered for the occasion and a deafening roar greeted the unfurling of the Congress flag by Pt. Nehru, the first Prime Minister of India.[1]

Independence Day was not only a day of triumph. It was also the prelude to a spectacle of barbaric cruelty, mass murder and wholesale migration.[2] Unlike many of his colleagues and Pakistani leaders, Nehru never succumbed to the communal mentality; throughout, he was the symbol of tolerance and reason.[3]

On Gandhiji's assassination on 30th January, 1948, this is how Nehru reacted, "friends and comrades, the light has gone out of our lives and there is darkness everywhere. I do not know what to tell you and how to say it. Our beloved leader, Bapu as we called him, the Father of the Nation, is no more".[4]

The Partition had released torrential forces of disorder which threatened to submerge the new Dominion at its birth: communal riots and mass migration; war in Kashmir; the danger of territorial fragmentation on a scale which few States in modern times have encountered; and economic dislocation. A new Constitution had to be framed, to embody the Congress pledges of a generation. That chaos was avoided primarily due to the leadership

1. Michael Brecher: A Political Biography of Nehru, pp. 355-356, published by Oxford University Press.
2. Michael Brecher: A Political Biography of Nehru, p. 358, published by Oxford University Press.
3. Michael Brecher: A Political Biography of Nehru, p. 365, published by Oxford University Press.
4. Michael Brecher: A Political Biography of Nehru, p. 386, published by Oxford University Press.

of Nehru and Patel who carried the full burden of decision affecting the fate of millions and the country at large.[1]

Pandit Nehru played an important role in the framing of the India's Constitution, which was formally adopted on 26th January, 1950. After the death of Sardar Patel by the end of 1950 there was a bitter struggle in the Congress Party. However, Pandit Jawaharlal Nehru retained his position as leader, and assumed Congress Presidency on 9th September, 1951. The 1951-52 Elections was a striking success and Congress won overwhelming majority of seats in Parliament. From 1951 to 1954, Pandit Jawaharlal Nehru remained President of the Congress.

Michael Brecher's Political Biography of Pandit Jawaharlal Nehru published by Oxford University Press in 1959 mentions that there have been four Indian Cabinets since 1947, all headed by Nehru and all composed largely of Congressmen. At no time has the Government been in danger from a vote of 'no-confidence', for the Congress has had an overwhelming majority in Parliament. The Cabinet system in India has brought a high degee of stability. This has been one of its distinguishing features. Another has been Nehru's pre-eminence.[2]

Pandit Jawaharlal Nehru led the Congress to a major victory in the 1957 Elections, but his Government was facing rising problems and criticism. Pandit Jawaharlal Nehru's Panch Shila, (five principles of peaceful co-existence), were greatly hailed and formed the basis of 1954 Sino-Indian Treaty over Tibet. However, in later years, Chinese invasion of North Eastern India exposed the weakness of India's military strength, and foreign policy. In the 1962 Elections, Nehru led the Congress to victory

1. Michael Brecher: A Political Biography of Nehru, p. 401, published by Oxford University Press.
2. Michael Brecher: A Political Biography of Nehru, p. 449, published by Oxford University Press.

but with diminished majority. Pandit Jawaharlal Nehru, symbol of Asia's political awakening, resolute fighter for national freedom, outstanding man of the age, and the first Prime Minister of Independent India left for his heavenly abode in the early hours of May 27, 1964, mourned by the entire nation and cremated at the Shantivan on the banks of Yamuna river.

Commemoration

In his life-time, Jawaharlal Nehru enjoyed an iconic status in India and was widely admired across the world for his idealism and statesmanship. His birthday, 14 November, is celebrated in India as *Children's Day* in recognition of his life-long passion and work for the welfare, education and development of children and young people. Children across India remember him as *Chacha Nehru* (Uncle Nehru). Nehru remains a popular symbol of the Congress Party which frequently celebrates his memory. Congress leaders and activists often emulate his style of clothing, especially the *Gandhi cap,* and his mannerisms. Nehru's ideals and policies continue to shape the Congress Party's manifesto and core political philosophy.

DR. BABASAHEB AMBEDKAR

(April 14, 1891 – December 6, 1956)

"Dr. Babasaheb Ambedkar was the Chairman of the Drafting Committee of the Constituent Assembly charged by the Assembly to write free India's Constitution and he has won accolades not only from his colleagues but also from all the contemporary and legal luminaries for his drafting work. He was a member of the Adoption of the National Flag Committee."

[1]Dr. Ambedkar also known as *Babasaheb,* was an Indian nationalist, jurist, Dalit, political leader, activist, philosopher, thinker, anthropologist, historian, orator, prolific writer, economist, scholar, editor, revolutionary and the revivalist of Buddhism in India. He was also the chief architect of the Indian Constitution. Born into a poor untouchable family, Ambedkar spent his whole life fighting against social discrimination, the system of *Chaturvarna* – the Hindu categorization of human society into four *varnas* – and the Indian caste system.

An eminent constitutional lawyer, an authority on economics and political issues, a statesman, an author, an agitator and an architect of the Indian Constitution, Dr. Bhimrao Ramji Ambedkar adorned diverse fields, but he will always be remembered as the unquestionable leader of the depressed classes.

---

1. The great Indians by One India One People Foundation in collaboration with Authorspress.

Bhimrao, born on April 14, 1891, in 'Mhow' village in Central India, he was affectionately called Bhima; and the name Bhimrao stuck to him after he completed his college studies. Like his grandfather, Maloji, Bhim's father, Ramji Sakpal, too was in the army of the British Government. In those days the British Government had made education compulsory for the men in the army. The Government also ran schools for their women and children. Both Maloji and Ramji, were indeed the rare and fortunate ones amongst the "Mahars' to have the benefits of education. At the age of five, Bhim joined a school in Dapoli. Bhim's forefathers originally belonged to a place called Ambavade in the Konkon region and it was while studying in Satara that Bhim acquired the surname 'Ambedkar'.

After marriage Bhimrao joined the Elphinstone College and continued with his studies. In college he was ridiculed for being a Mahar. He was anguished to see all around the 'untouchables' being ill-treated similarly. During the course of his college studies, Bhimrao continued to read incessantly. He completed his Intermediate course. It was beyond Ramji's means to bear the cost of Bhim's further education. Fortunately, the Maharaja of Baroda, Sayaji Rao Gaikwad, granted a scholarship that enabled Bhimrao to attain the degree of Bachelor of Arts in 1912.

After the death of his father, Ramji, the responsibility of the entire family rested on Bhimrao's young shoulders. Once again Sayaji Rao, the Maharaja of Baroda, came to his rescue and selected him to be sent to America for his higher studies in return for serving the State of Baroda for ten years. He wrote a thesis on 'Ancient Indian Commerce' and, in 1915, acquired the Master of Arts degree and also wrote another thesis on 'National Dividend for India, a Historical and Analytical study' which was accepted by the Columbia University in 1916 and Ambedkar was awarded a Doctorate of Philosophy.

At this time the Baroda Government decided to terminate his scholarship and hence he was forced to return to India. As per the agreement with Sayaji Rao, the Maharaja of Baroda, he completed the remaining years of service with them at Baroda. Thereafter, he returned to Bombay in 1917, to serve as a lecturer in Sydenham College with the aim to save money for completion of his higher studies.

In 1920, Ambedkar went back to London and completed his studies and returned to India. Now he was a Barrister. He set up an organization known as 'Bahishkrit Hitakarini Sabha'. He started free schools for the young generation with reading rooms and libraries. He became a father figure to the poor and low class people. They started calling him "Baba" and more respectfully as "Babasaheb." He told them to attain self-elevation with self-help and regain self-respect by gaining self-knowledge. According to the Simon Commission's recommendation, the British government invited various leaders from various parts for discussion to England, to attend the Round Table Conference. Dr. Ambedkar was also invited to represent the cause of the untouchables. Mahatma Gandhi too participated in this meeting. In November 1932, Dr. Ambedkar attended the third session of the Round Table Conference. In August 1936, he established his own political party with the name "Independent Labour Party". The elections took place on February 17, 1937. Dr. Ambedkar with many of his members won this election with majority.

Fight against untouchability

As a leading Indian scholar, Ambedkar had been invited to testify before the Southborough Committee, which was preparing the Government of India Act, 1919. At this hearing, Ambedkar argued for creating separate electorates and reservations for Dalits and other religious communities. In 1920, he began the publication of the weekly *Mooknayak (Leader of the Silent)* in Mumbai. Attaining popularity, Ambedkar used this journal to criticize orthodox Hindu politicians and a perceived reluctance of the Indian political community to fight caste discrimination. His speech at a Depressed Classes Conference in Kolhapur impressed the local State ruler Shahu IV, who shocked orthodox society by dining with Ambedkar. Ambedkar established a successful legal practice, and also organised the Bahishkrit Hitakarini Sabha to promote education and socio-economic uplifting of the depressed classes. In 1926, he became a nominated member of the Bombay Legislative Council. And also he formed a social organization on 25th November, 1926. for social security. He gave help to retired Ex-Servicemen from Mahar Regiment which was a great job in First World War and also importance of discipline was understood and as proved by the British in India without discipline no rule would have been possible on the Indians and to change the mentality of common men about untouchability. The upper caste people put lot of restrictions on untouchables. By 1927 Dr. Ambedkar decided to launch active movements against untouchability. He began with public movements and marches to open up and share public drinking water resources, also he began a struggle for the right to enter Hindu temples. He led a *satyagraha* in Mahad to fight for the right of the untouchable community to draw water from the main water tank of the town.

He was appointed to the Bombay Presidency Committee to work with the all-European Simon Commission in 1928. This Commission had sparked great protests across India, and while its report was ignored by most Indians, Ambedkar himself wrote a separate set of recommendations for future constitutional reformers.

The Viceroy of India appointed him on the Defence Advisory Committee in July 1941. Mahatma Gandhi launched the 'Quit India' movement of August 9, 1942 with a "Do or Die" spirit. By this time the British Government realized that it was no longer possible for them to keep India in bondage. At the very moment Dr. Ambedkar, founded the people's Educational Society and the society opened its first college known as "Siddharth College".

As per the Cabinet Mission, members were elected by Provincial Legislative Assemblies to form a Constituent Assembly who were to frame the Constitution. Dr. Ambedkar was brought into the Constituent Assembly with the backing from the Scheduled Castes and with support from the Muslim League. In April 1947 he submitted to the Assembly a draft on "States and Minorities". The Constituent Assembly, on April 29, 1947 declared that untouchability in all forms would be abolished in India. The British Parliament passed the Act of Indian Independence on July 15, 1947 and immediately after that the first Cabinet Ministry of Free India was formed and Dr. Ambedkar was invited to join the Cabinet as the Law Minister, which he accepted.

On August 15, 1947 India became Independent. Dr. Ambedkar was called to draft the Constitution of Independent India whereby he was appointed as the Chairperson. He completed this vast and varied work in February, 1948.

Upon India's Independence on August 15, 1947, the new Congress-led government invited Ambedkar to serve as the nation's first Law Minister, which he accepted. On August 29, Ambedkar was appointed Chairman of the Constitution Drafting Committee, charged by the Assembly to write free India's new Constitution. Ambedkar won great praise from his colleagues and contemporary observers for his drafting work.

The text prepared by Ambedkar provided constitutional guarantees and protections for a wide range of civil liberties for individual citizens, including freedom of religion, the abolition of untouchability and the outlawing of all forms of discrimination. Ambedkar argued for extensive economic and social rights for women, and also won the Assembly's support for introducing a system of reservations of jobs in the civil services, schools and colleges for members of Scheduled Castes and Scheduled Tribes, a system akin to affirmative action. India's lawmakers hoped to eradicate the socio-economic inequalities and lack of opportunities for India's depressed classes through this measure, which had been originally envisioned as temporary on a need basis. The Constitution was adopted on November 26, 1949 by the Constituent Assembly.

Around this time news arrived from United States of America that the famous Columbia University had awarded the Doctorate of Law degree to Dr. Ambedkar. Dr. Ambedkar went to New York to receive it on June 5, 1952. Age and ill-health did not deter Ambedkar from working non-stop. When he realized that the Hindu Society would never grant social equality to his people, he started looking for an alternate religion, which would make his dream come true. A religion where every man was treated as an equal. He found his answer in Buddhism. After deliberating for a long-time and after studying several other religions he finally embraced Buddhism on October 14, 1956.

Dr. Ambedkar was a well-known author and finally completed his book, "The Buddha and his Gospel". He also completed two more books, "Revolutions and Counter-revolutions in India" and "The Buddha and Karl Marx". Although he was a highly controversial figure, he played a very constructive and a very important role in the making of Constitution of India and Hindu Law reforms. By 1956, when he died, he had succeeded in raising his caste fellows from the dust to the dignity of an equal citizenship. Today in India all the temples, public places are open to the depressed classes. Ambedkar attained "Nirvana" on December 6, 1956 and was posthumously awarded "The Bharat Ratna" in the year 1990.

SACHCHIDANANDA SINHA

(1871-1950)

"He was the oldest member of the Assembly and the first elected provisional Chairman of the Constituent Assembly, elected on 9th December, 1946. Shri J.B. Kriplani, the then Congress President requested Shri Sachchidananda Sinha to take the chair of the Constituent Assembly. He delivered his first inaugural address and made comparison of various Constitutions of the world and made a dynamic call to the Constituent Assembly, on the occasion of its first meeting."

Born in a respectable middle-class Kayastha family at Arrah, the headquarters of the Shahabad district in Bihar, on 10 November, 1871, Sachchidananda was the youngest child (and the only son in the family) of Bakshi Ramyad Sinha, the Chief Pleader of the Maharaja of Dumraon. His grandfather, Bakshi Shiva Prasad had been the Diwan of the Dumraon Estate.

From his parents Sachchidananda inherited a sprit of rationalism which gave him the strength to rebel openly in later life against unjust social restrictions and meaningless religious rituals and superstitions.

Sachchidananda became the recognized spokesman of the Bihari people and was chosen Secretary of the Reception Committee of the Congress session at Bankipore (Patna) in 1912. He was the President of the Bihar Provincial Congress Committee during 1916-20.

He founded the Hindustan Review in 1901, which he edited till his death except during the years 1921-26 when he was an Executive Councillor of Bihar and Orissa in charge of Jails, Judiciary and Finance. He was the first Indian to hold the Finance Portfolio in a Province.

Sachchidananda was educated at the Arrah Zilla School, T.K. Ghosh Academy at Patna, Patna College and City College, Calcutta. While he was a first-year Arts student of the Patna College, in 1888, he was deeply impressed by what he heard of and read about the genius and activities of Pandit Madan Mohan Malaviya.

In September 1919 Sachchidananda was elected to the Imperial Legislative Council and was its first elected Deputy President. In 1921 at the request of Lord Sinha, Governor of Bihar and Orissa, he became an Executive Councillor (1921-26) and also acted as President of the Bihar and Orissa Legislative Council from July 1921 to November 1922.

Sachchidananda presided over the 35th session of the All India Kayastha Conference at Delhi in 1929. Next year he was elected unopposed from his home constituency of Shahabad to the Bihar and Orissa Legislative Council and became the leader of the opposition until 1937.

While in England he assisted the Congress Delegation of 1890 led by George Yule and worked as a volunteer for the election of Dadabhai Naoroji from the central Finsbury consistency in 1892. The training in practical politics, he thus received, stood him in good stead when he himself entered Indian Politics as a Congressman in 1894.

Sachchidananda was called to the Bar from the Middle Temple on 26 January 1893 and returned to India in March.

To agitate for the creation of a separate province of Bihar he started a journal, the Bihar Times, at Patna in 1894 with Mahesh Narayan as its Editor. The movement move particularly after the partition of Bengal in 1905. In 1906 he reconstituted the management of the Bihar Times and changed its name to the Beharee to serve the local interests best.

In 1946 he was elected by the Bihar Legislative Council to the Constituent Assembly of India and he presided over its inaugural session.

Because of his valuable services to the nation, honours began to pour profusely on him. The degree of Doctor of Letters (*honoris causa*) was conferred on him by the Allahabad University in 1937, by the Patna University in 1947 and by the Benares Hindu University in 1948. Earlier, in 1944, the Governor of Bihar, Sir Thomas Rutherford, proposed his name for Knighthood, but he declined to accept it because he considered democratic ideals and acceptance of official titles incompatible.

Almost the last act of Sachchidananda was his signing on 14 February 1950, at a special function arranged by President Rajendra Prasad, the Indian Constitution after it had been finally adopted by the Constituent Assembly.

His book, 'Some Eminent' were attributed to him. But he remained steadfast.

In administration – whether in the Government, in the University or in any other public organisation – he endeared himself to the people all the more by his boldness, impartiality, punctuality and hard work, and throughout his public life all sections of the public were attracted to him by his charity, hospitality and personality.

DIWAN BAHADUR ALLADI

Krishnaswamy Ayyar

(14 May 1883 – 3 October 1953)

"Sir Diwan Bahadur Alladi Krishnaswamy Ayyar, Advocate-General of Madras State was a member of the Constituent Assembly of India which was responsible for framing the Constitution of India. He was also the Chairman of the Credential Committee, Member of Rules Committee and the member of All India Women Conference."

SIR ALLADI KRISHNASWAMY AYYAR was an Indian lawyer and member of the Constituent Assembly of India, which was responsible for framing the Constitution of India. He was Advocate-General of the Composite Madras State.

Alladi Krishnaswamy Ayyar was born in 1883 in the small village of Pudur in Nellore district of Andhra Pradesh. His father Ekamra Sastry, a priest, was content to spend his days in peace and piety. Even so, he ensured his son Krishnaswamy was educated. Krishnaswamy was a meritorious student and after passing his matriculation examination in 1899, he joined the Madras Christian College to study history. Alladi used his spare time to attend classes in law and passed the B.L. exam and became the leader of the Bar in seven years, a position he retained throughout his life. He was made a Dewan Bahadur in 1930 and was knighted in the 1932 New Year Honours List.

Alladi Memorial Trust was founded in 1983 by Alladi Kuppuswami to commemorate the birth centenary of his father Alladi Krishnaswamy Ayyar. It is aimed to help poor litigants, lawyers and students of law and for helping in the administration of justice. Alladi Memorial Lectures are delivered every year on issues relating to the Indian Constitution. The lecturers are Justice V.R. Krishna Iyer, Justice Y.V. Chandrachud, Sri P.C. Rao, Sri Pavani Parameswara Rao, Nandita Haksar, Rama Devi and Justice M. Jagannadha Rao.

BENEGAL NARSING RAU

(B. 26 February 1887 Mangalore,
d. 30 November 1953)

"Sir Benegal Narsing Rau was the India's representative to the United States Security Council. He is known for his key role in drafting of the Constitution of India. He was appointed as the Constitution Advisor to the members of the Union Constitutional Committee and the Provincial Constitution Committee."

Sir Benegal Narsing Rau CIE or **B.N. Rau** was an Indian bureaucrat, jurist, diplomat and statesman known for his key role in drafting the Constitution of India. He was also India's representative to the United Nations Security Council from 1950 to 1952. He was the brother of former Governor of Reserve Bank of India Benegal Rama Rau.

One of the foremost Indian jurists of his time, he helped draft the Constitutions of Burma (Myanmar) in 1947 and India in 1950. As India's representative on the United Nations Security Council (1950–52), he was serving as president of the council when it recommended armed assistance to South Korea (June 1950). Later he was a member of the Korean War post United Nations Command Military Armistice Commission (UNCMAC).

A graduate of the Universities of Madras and Cambridge, Rau entered the Indian Civil Services in 1910.

After revising the entire Indian statutory code (1935–37), he was knighted (1938) and made judge (1939) of the Bengal High Court at Calcutta (Kolkatta). His writings on Indian law include a noted study on constitutional precedents as well as articles on human rights in India. He served briefly (1944-45) as Prime Minister of Jammu and Kashmir State. From February 1952 until his death, he was a Judge of the Permanent Court of International Justice, The Hague. Before his election to the court, he was regarded as a candidate for Secretary-General of the United Nations.

Narsing Rau was born in Mangalore on 26 February 1887 in a family of intellectuals. His father Benegal Raghavendra Rau was an eminent doctor. Narsing Rau passed Matriculation in 1901 from the Canara High School, Mangalore, topping the list of students of the entire Madras Presidency. He stood first in the entire University in the F.A. (Intermediate) examination and gained his degree with First Class marks in English, Sanskrit, and Mathematics. On a scholarship, he proceeded to Trinity College, Cambridge, and took his Tripos in 1909, just missing, the Senior Wranglership.

B.N. Rau passed the Indian Civil Service Examination in 1909 and returned to India, posted to Bengal. Doing well on the Executive side, in 1909 he moved to the Judiciary. His distinguished work brought him a Knighthood in 1938. Rau retired from service in 1944.

After retirement from the Indian Civil Services, Rau was appointed as the Prime Minister of the princely State of Jammu and Kashmir.

B.N. Rau was appointed as the Constitutional Adviser to the Constituent Assembly in formulating the Indian Constitution. He was responsible for the general structure of the democratic framework of the Constitution and prepared its original draft.

The Constituent Assembly's resolution setting up the Drafting Committee, under the chairmanship of B.R. Ambedkar, declared that it was being set up to "Scrutinise the Draft of the text of the Constitution prepared by the Constitutional Adviser giving effect to the decisions taken already in the Assembly and including all matters ancillary thereto or which have to be provided in such a Constitution, and to submit to the Assembly for consideration the text of the Draft Constitution as revised by the Committee. There already was a Draft in existence when this Committee was set up.

The President of the Constituent Assembly Dr. Rajendra Prasad, before signing the Constitution on 26 November, 1949, thanked Rau for having 'worked honorarily all the time that he was here, assisting the Assembly not only with his knowledge and erudition but also enabled the other members to perform their duties with thoroughness and intelligence by supplying them with the material on which they could work. B.N. Rau was not a member of the Assembly but was perhaps as important in the framing of the Constitution.

Rau served India as a representing delegate in the United Nations. From 1949 to 1952 he was India's Permanent Representative to the U.N., till he was appointed as a Judge of the International Court in The Hague. He also served as the President of the United Nations Security Council in 1950.

K.M. MUNSHI

(30 Dec., 1887 – 9 Feb., 1971)

"K.M. Munshi was an elected member of the Bombay Legislative Assembly and was the first Home Minister of the Congress Government in Bombay Presidency. He has played an important role in framing of the Indian Constitution and he was also the member on the Flag Committee that selected the flag of India in 1947. He was also the member of the Order of Business Committee, elected to the Expert Committee to Constituent Assembly, Members of Rules of Procedure Committee, Steering Committee, Order of Business Committee & Adoption of the National Flag Committee."

[1]K.M. Munshi a dynamic 'Kulapati' was widely described as a man of great ideas and indomitable courage. He had a multi-faceted personality.

Kanhaiyalal Maneklal Munshi was born at Bharuch on December 30, 1887. He studied at Baroda College where under the influence of Sri Aurobindo, he was attracted to the idea of armed rebellion against the British rule. Also a bright student, Munshi performed brilliantly in his B.A. and LL.B. exams.

By 1913, Munshi had become a full-fledged advocate. He moved to Bombay and joined Annie Besant's All India Home Rule League. In 1917, Munshi became a member of

1. The great Indians by One India One People Foundation in collaboration with Authorspress.

the Subjects Committee of the Indian National Congress. In 1920, he resigned from the Congress and the Home Rule League to devote himself to liberty activities and law. About this time his first novel was being serialized in a Gujarati weekly. In 1927, he was elected to the Bombay Legislative Council and played a leading role in piloting the Bombay University Bill. He took an active part in the Civil Disobedience Movement and the Salt *Satyagraha* launched by Gandhiji. In 1932 he was sentenced to two years' rigorous imprisonment. K.M. Munshi has played an important role in the freedom struggle. His name will be remembered along with other eminent lawyers, who made sacrifices for the liberation of the country from foreign rule.

In 1937, with the implementation of the Government of India Act, 1935, Munshi was elected as a member of the Bombay Legislative Assembly. He was the first Home Minister of the Congress Government that was sworn in Bombay Presidency.

On November 8, 1938, he founded the Bharatiya Vidya Bhavan and became its first Kulpati. The same year he founded the Institute of Agriculture at Anand. Bharatiya Vidya Bhavan's prime object was the propagation of the enduring values of Indian culture. Apart from his association with Bharatiya Vidya Bhavan he was associated with numerous cultural, social and academic bodies.

To the present generation he would be known as the Food and Agriculture Minister during 1950, and subsequently as former Governor of Uttar Pradesh. Munshi is, however, most remembered for his efforts to promote education in India.

He was a prolific writer and conscientious journalist. Munshi launched a Gujarati monthly called Bhargava. He was joint-editor of Young India and started the

Bhavan's Journal in 1954. He is reckoned as one of the luminaries of Gujarati literature and established his reputation as an outstanding novelist.

After the independence of India, Munshi was appointed the diplomatic envoy and trade agent to the Princely State of Hyderabad, where he served until its accession in 1948. Munshi was on the *ad hoc* Flag Committee that selected the Flag of India in August 1947, and on the committee which drafted the Constitution of India under the chairmanship of Dr. B.R. Ambedkar. He and Purushottam Das Tandon were among those who strongly opposed propagation and conversion in the Constituent Assembly. He was also the main driving force behind the renovation of the historically important Somnath Temple by the Government of India just after independence.

He served as the Governor of Indian State of Uttar Pradesh from 1952 to 1957. In 1959, Munshi separated from the Nehru-dominated Congress Party and joined the newly formed Swatantra Party led by Chakravarti Rajgopalachari, which was right-wing in its politics and pro-business, pro-free market economy and private property rights. The party enjoyed limited success, but eventually died out. Later, Munshi joined the Jan Sangh.

Besides being a politician and educator, K.M. Munshi was also an environmentalist. He initiated the Vanmahotsav in 1950, when he was Union Minister of Agriculture and Food, to increase the area under forest cover. Since then Van Mahotsav a week-long festival of tree plantation is organised every year in the month of July all across the country and lakhs of trees are planted.

Munshi was also a litterateur with a wide range of interests. He is well-known for his historical novels in Gujarati, especially his trilogy *Patanni Prabhuta* (The Greatness of Patan), *Gujaratno Nath* (The Ruler of Gujarat) and *Rajadhiraj* (The Emperor). His other works include *Jay Somnath, Krishnavatara, Bhagavan Parasurama,* and *Tapasvini* (The Lure of Power) a novel with a fictional parallel drawn from the Freedom Movement of India under Mahatma Gandhi.

K.M. Munshi's novel *Prithvi Vallabh* was made into a movie of the same name twice. The adaptation directed by Manilal Joshi in 1924 was very controversial in its day: Mahatma Gandhi rallied against it for excessive sex and violence. The second version was by Sohrab Modi in 1943.

Munshi passed away on February 9, 1971. The Bharatiya Vidya Bhavan is engaged in its mission of continuously propagating what Indian culture is all about, with many branches in India and abroad, and would be a constant reminder of the prominent role played by K.M. Munshi in the freedom struggle.

T.T. KRISHNAMACHARI

(1899 – 1974)

"T.T. Krishnamachari has played an important role in drafting the Constitution of India and he was a prominent member of the Drafting Committee and was responsible for building the economic and industrial infrastructure of the country."

Tiruvellore Thattai Krishnamachari or T.T. Krishnamachari, was a man most noted for being the Finance Minister of the Union Government of India. T.T. Krishnamachari, however, distinguished himself as an economics genius and this was mostly because he enjoyed not one, but two terms of power as the Finance Minister of India. As far as his name goes, he was popularly known as TTK and hardly ever referred to as Tiruvellore Thattai Krishnamachari. As a politician, T.T. Krishnamachari owed his loyalties to the 'Indian National Congress' and he remained faithful to this party to the very end. Many people know that T.T. Krishnamachari was the Finance Minister of India, but not too many people that he was also a visiting professor at the 'Department of Economics' in 'Madras Christian College'. Apart from being noted for being the national Finance Minister, T.T. Krishnamachari was also recognized for being the member of the drafting committee, a successful entrepreneur and a prominent Congress leader.

Not too many details are known about the early life of Tiruvellore Thattai Krishnamachari but, from what is known, it is easy to establish that he was born into a Tamil Brahmin family. Post his initial years of schooling, T.T. Krishnamachari went on to study and graduate from the Madras Christian College or MCC as it is popularly known.

T.T. Krishnamachari was mostly known for being one of the most prominent founders of modern India. He proved extremely helpful in drafting the Constitution as a very prominent member of the 'Drafting Committee' and also helped build the economic and industrial infrastructure of the country. Such accomplishments, under no means, can be considered ordinary. Speaking strictly in terms of a career, T.T. Krishnamachari began his career as a businessman, in the strictest sense of the term. He started off small, but went on to plant the foundation of the vastly successfully consumer goods firm called "TT Krishnamachari & Co." in 1928 in Chennai. The business he established is now popularly known as the 'TTK Group' and deals with a wide array of products including kitchenware, personal care, pharmaceuticals, medical devices, baby care, etc. Soon after the company began to flourish, in spite of the competition, T.T. Krishnamachari shifted his focus to politics, and hereto he managed to earn an enviable reputation for himself.

For T.T. Krishnamachari, it all began when he was initially elected to the 'Madras Legislative Assembly' as an independent member. From here on there was no looking back for him and he went on to join the 'Indian National Congress'. In 1946, he was made a part of the 'Constituent Assembly' at the Centre. From 1952 to 1965, he enjoyed the responsibility of being Central Minister twice. He was made the first Minster of Commerce and Industry and then actually went to become the Finance Minister.

Apart from the key positions mentioned above, T.T. Krishnamachari was made and remained incharge of the steel ministry for a considerable amount of time. He became minister again in 1962, but this time around he was not handed any portfolio. But within a short span of time, he was made the Minister for Economic and Defence Corporation. Right after this responsibility was given to him, it was withdrawn and T.T. Krishnamachari was made the Finance Minister for the second time.

As far as achievements are concerned, T.T. Krishnamachari had quite a lot of them under his belt. He proved to be extremely useful in the setting up of some of India's biggest steel plants. This notwithstanding, he also played a very prominent role in the setting up of financial institutions like IDBI, UTI and ICICI in the country. During his two stints as the Finance Minister of India, T.T Krishnamachari introduced quite a number of path breaking reforms that, to this very day, are still looked up to.

In spite of being as active as he was in politics, T.T. Krishnamachari decided to hang his gloves for good when he resigned from the post of 'Minister' in 1965. This he did when his term as 'Member of Parliament' was over. After bidding adieu to politics, he continued to lead an intellectually stimulating life. Not once did he make it seem like he resigned from his important post for recreational purposes. Sadly however, age and illnesses caught up with T.T. Krishnamachari and he breathed his last in 1974.

HANSA MEHTA

(Birth – 3 July, 1897)

"Hansa Mehta was the member of the Constituent Assembly of India. She had the privilege of presenting the National Flag to the Nation on behalf of the Women of India. She represented India on the Executive Board of UNESCO."

She was a prolific orator and freedom fighter who made it her mission to free India.

Hansa Mehta was an educationist and she was the first woman to be appointed Vice-Chancellor of a co-education University in India. She was a prolific-writer and an orator. She was a freedom fighter who made it her mission to free India. She actively took part in the freedom struggle and had to suffer imprisonment many a times. She was known as the dictator of Bombay.

Hansa Mehta was born on 3rd July, 1897 at Surat in a Nagar Grahasta family that was well-known for their liberal views, scholarship and administrative capabilities. She was the daughter of Manubhai Mehta who started his career as Professor of Philosophy in Baroda College rose through ability and merit to be the prime minister of Baroda State. She was sent to school and college in Baroda. She graduated from the Baroda College, and then affiliated to the Bombay University, with B.A. (Hons) in Philosophy. She and her older sister, Jayashri Raiji were the third among Gujarati women to obtain a college degree. She sailed for England to study journalism.

In London she met Mrs. Sarojini Naidu and it was Mrs. Naidu who initiated Hansaben into the women's movement by taking her to meetings. Later she sailed to U.S.A alone. There she attended educational and social work conferences and met women active in suffragette movement.

Hansaben came under the influence of Gandhiji and joined India's national freedom movement. She organized picketing of shops selling foreign clothes as well as liquor shops, and participated in other freedom movement activities. As the dictator of Bombay she led a mammoth procession which was joined by Sardar Vallabhbhai Patel, Maulana Abdul Kalam Azad and some other Congress working committee members. At her presidential address at the All-India Women's Conference convention held in Hyderabad, Hansaben proposed a Charter of Women's Rights. The Charter proved useful in clarifying the woman's status and pressing for suitable legislation regarding the same. The first such legislation that was taken up was the codification of the Hindu Law.

Hansaben was a member of the Constituent Assembly of India. On the historic occasion of the transfer of power, she had the privilege of presenting the National flag to the nation on behalf of the women of India. On the International scene, Hansaben represented India on the Nuclear Sub-Commission, on the Status of Women in the United Nations. She represented India on the Executive Board of UNESCO and led Indian delegations to several international conferences. In India, she was associated with many educational, social and cultural organizations. In recognition of her contribution to social service, Hansaben was awarded the Padma Bhushan.

N. GOPALASWAMI AYYANGAR

(1882 - 1953)

N. Gopalaswami Ayyangar was leader of Rajya Sabha and a minister in Government of India. He joined the Madras civil service in 1905 and rose to become Collector. He served as Prime minister of Kashmir from 1937 to 1943. He was Knighted by the British government.

An able administrator, Ayyangar was a member of the Rules, Business, Drafting and several other committees. Ayyangar played a key role in the exposition of Article 370 and was responsible for closing the differences between Sardar Patel and Sheikh Abdullah.

Coming from a distinguished family, Ayyangar was born and educated at Madras. Beginning as a professor, he entered the Civil Service and for over thirty years served in various responsible capacities, as Collector, Registrar-General of Panchayats, Secretary of P.W.D and Member, Revenue Board. Seeking retirement in 1937, he took over the Premiership of Kashmir State and concerned himself with the all-round development of the valley. Later, elected to the Council of States, he served the Committee for the Indiansation of Army as its Chairman.

A co-author of the Sapru Committee Report, Ayyangar was one of the architects of the Indian Constitution and proved himself an asset to the Constitution Assembly and its Draft Committee. In 1947, he joined the Dominion

Government as a Prime Minister without Portfolio and later took over the Ministry of Transport and Railways. He was successful restoring the rail system, after the tremendous strain of the war years, to pre-war efficiency. Succeeding Sardar Patel in 1950, he took charge of the Ministry of States and fulfilled Sardar Patel's mission by accomplishing the task of the integration of the States. Later he served as the Defence Minister.

An authority over Kashmir affairs, Ayyangar presented India's case in United Nations and led the Indian delegation to various conferences. Ayyangar to the present generation is an unsung hero who contributed to the making of the Constitution.

RAJKUMARI AMRIT KAUR

(2 February, 1889 – 2 October, 1964)

"Rajkumari Amrit Kaur was the first woman to hold the rank of Cabinet Minister during the first Cabinet of Pandit Jawaharlal Nehru. She was the first Asian woman to hold the post of the President of the World Health Organization. She was the woman member elected to the Constituent Assembly. She was also the Chairman of the Finance Staff Committee."

Rajkumari Amrit Kaur was the Health Minister in the Indian Cabinet for ten years after India's independence from the British Raj in 1947. She was an eminent Gandhian, a freedom fighter, and a social activist.

The Rajkumari was born on 2 February, 1889 in Lucknow, Uttar Pradesh (then United Provinces), India. She and her seven brothers were the eight children of Raja Harnam Singh, a member of the princely family of *Kapurthala* in the Punjab region.

The Rajkumari had her early education in Sherborne School for Girls in Dorset, England, and had her college education at Oxford University. After completing her education in England, she returned to India.

Participation in India's Freedom Movement

Raja Harnam Singh enjoyed the confidence of many Indian National Congress (INC) party leaders, including Gopal Krishna Gokhale. After her return to India from

England, Rajkumari got interested in India's freedom struggle through the occasional visits of those leaders to her father's home. After meeting in person Mahatma Gandhi in 1919 in Bombay (Mumbai), she felt drawn to his thoughts and vision for the country. The notorious *Jallianwala Bagh massacre* of mostly Sikhs the same year by the British Raj troops convinced her of the necessity of India's gaining its freedom from the Raj. She joined the INC, and began to participate in India's struggle for freedom, and also in social reform activities in India.

Rajkumari co-founded the All India Women's Conference in 1927, became its Secretary in 1930, and President in 1933.

For her participation in Gandhi-led 240-mile Dandi March in 1930, British Raj authorities imprisoned her.

Rajkumari went to live at Mahatma Gandhi's ashram in 1934, and took up the austere life there despite her aristocratic background. She served as one of Gandhi's secretaries for sixteen years.

As a representative of the INC, in 1937 Rajkumari went on a mission of goodwill to Bannu, in the present day Khyber-Pakhtunkhwa. The British Raj authorities charged her with sedition and imprisoned her.

In 1942, she participated in the Quit India Movement, and the British authorities imprisoned her again.

Rajkumari championed the cause of universal suffrage, and testified before the *Lothian Committee* on Indian franchise and constitutional reforms, and before the *Joint Select Committee of British Parliament* on Indian constitutional reforms.

Rajkumari served as the Chairperson of the All-India Women's Education Fund Association. She was a member of the Executive Committee of Lady Irwin College in New Delhi. The British Raj appointed her as a member of the Advisory Board of Education; (she resigned from that

Board during the Quit India Movement). She was sent as a member of the Indian delegation to UNESCO conferences in London and Paris in 1945 and 1946, respectively. She also served as a member of the Board of Trustees of the *All India Spinners' Association*.

Rajkumari worked to reduce illiteracy, and eradicate the custom of child marriages and the *purdah* system for women, which were prevalent then among some Indian communities.

After India's independence, Amrit Kaur became part of Jawaharlal Nehru's first Cabinet; she was the first woman to hold Cabinet rank. She was assigned the Ministry of Health and was one of only two Indian Christians in the Cabinet (along with John Mathai). In 1950, she was elected the president of World Health Organization, becoming the first woman and the first Asian to hold that post; for the first 25 years of that organisation's history, only two women held that post.

Kaur was a strong moving force behind the establishment of the *All India Institute of Medical Sciences* in New Delhi, and became its first president. For establishing the institute, she secured aid from New Zealand, Australia, West Germany, Sweden, and USA. She and one of her brothers donated their ancestral property and house (named *Manorville*) in Simla, Himachal Pradesh to serve as a holiday home for the staff and nurses of the Institute.

Kaur served as the Chairperson of the Indian Red Cross society for fourteen years. During her leadership, the Indian Red Cross did a number of pioneering works in the hinterlands of India. She initiated the *Tuberculosis Association of India* and the *Central Leprosy Teaching and Research Institute* in Madras (Chennai). She started the *Rajkumari Amrit Kaur College of Nursing* and the *National Sports Club of India*.

From 1957 until her death in 1964, she remained a member of Rajya Sabha. Between 1958 and 1963 Kaur was the president of the All-India Motor Transport Congress in Delhi. Until her death, she continued to be the President of the *All India Institute of Medical Sciences,* the *Tuberculosis Association of India,* and the *St. John's Ambulance Corps.* She also was awarded the *Rene Sand Memorial Award.*

Today, her private papers are part of the Archives at the Nehru Memorial Museum & Library, at Teen Murti House, New Delhi.

SAROJINI NAIDU

(13 February, 1879 – 2 March, 1949)

"She was popularly known as the nightingale of India and was the second woman who became the President of the Indian National Congress. She was also the Governor of the Uttar Pradesh. She was the woman member of the Constituent Assembly. She was the member of the All India Women's Conference, and Committee for Adoption of the National Flag."

SAROJINI NAIDU, also known by the sobriquet The Nightingale of India (Bharatiya Kokila), was a child prodigy, Indian independence activist and poet. Naidu was the second Indian woman to become the President of the Indian National Congress and the first woman to become the Governor of Uttar Pradesh State. Her birthday is celebrated as Women's Day in India.

Sarojini Chattopadhyay, later Naidu, belonged to Bengali family of Kulin Brahmins. She was born in Hyderabad, India as the eldest daughter of scientist, philosopher, linguist and educator Aghornath Chattopadhyaya and Varada Sundari Devi, a Bengali poetess. After receiving a doctor of science degree from Edinburgh University, her father settled in Hyderabad State, where he founded and administered the Hyderabad College, which later became the Nizam College in Hyderabad. Her father was a linguist and thinker, and the first member of Indian National Congress in Hyderabad.

Sarojini Naidu was the eldest among the eight siblings. One of her brothers Birendranath was a revolutionary and her other brother Harindranath was a poet, dramatist, and actor.

Education

Sarojini Naidu was a brilliant student. She was proficient in Urdu, Telugu, English, Bengali and Persian. At the age of twelve, Sarojini Naidu attained national fame when she topped the matriculation examination at Madras University. Her father wanted her to become a mathematician or scientist but Sarojini Naidu was interested in poetry. She started writing poems in English. Impressed by her play *Maher Muneer*, the Nizam of Hyderabad gave her scholarship to study abroad. At the age of 16, she travelled to England to study first at King's College, London and later at Girton College, Cambridge.

Gandhi in London with Sarojini Naidu at his side joined the Indian national movement in the wake of partition of Bengal in 1905. She came into contact with Gopal Krishna Gokhale, Rabindranath Tagore, Muhammad Ali Jinnah, Annie Besant, C.P. Ramaswami Iyer, Mahatma Gandhi and Jawaharlal Nehru.

During 1915-1918, she travelled to different regions in India delivering lectures on social welfare, women empowerment, and nationalism. She awakened the women of India and brought them out of the kitchen. She also helped to establish the Women's Indian Association (WIA) in 1917. She was sent to London along with Annie Besant, President of WIA, to present the case for the women's vote to the Joint Select Committee. She was woman member of the Constituent Assembly and played eminent role in the committee constituted by the president of the Constituent Assembly.

In 1925, Sarojini Naidu presided over the annual session of Indian National Congress at Kanpur. In 1929, she presided over East African Indian Congress in South Africa. She was awarded the Kaiser-i-Hind medal by the British government for her work during the plague epidemic in India. In 1930, she participated in the Round table conference with Gandhiji and Madan Mohan Malaviya. Sarojini Naidu played a leading role during the Civil Disobedience Movement and was jailed along with Gandhiji and other leaders. In 1942, Sarojini Naidu was arrested during the "Quit India" movement and was jailed for 21 months with Gandhiji. She shared a very warm relationship with Gandhiji and used to call him "Mickey Mouse".

Sarojini Naidu was moved by the partition of Bengal in 1905 and decided to join the Indian freedom struggle. She met regularly Gopal Krishna Gokhale, who later introduced her to the stalwarts of the Indian freedom movement. She met Mahatma Gandhi, Pandit Jawaharlal Nehru, C.P. Ramaswami Iyer and Muhammad Ali Jinnah. With such an encouraging environment, Sarojini later moved on to become leader of the Indian National Congress Party. She travelled extensively to the United States of America and many European countries as the flag-bearer of the Indian Nationalist struggle.

During 1915, Sarojini Naidu travelled all over India and delivered speeches on welfare of youth, dignity of labour, women's emancipation and nationalism. In 1916, she took up the cause of the indigo workers of Champaran in the western district of Bihar.

In March 1919, the British government passed the Rowlatt Act by which the possession of seditious documents was deemed illegal. Mahatma Gandhi organized the Non-Cooperation Movement to protest and Naidu was the first to join the movement. Besides, Sarojini

Naidu also actively campaigned for the Montagu-Chelmsford Reforms, the Khilafat issue, the Sabarmati Pact, the Satyagraha Pledge and the Civil Disobedience Movement.

In 1919, she went to England as a member of the All-India Home Rule Deputation. In January 1924, she was one of the two delegates of the Indian National Congress Party to attend the East African Indian Congress. In 1925, she was elected as the President of the Indian National Congress Party.

Sarojini Naidu was the first woman Governor of Uttar Pradesh. Her chairmanship of the Asian Relations Conference in 1947 was highly-appraised. Two years later, on 2 March 1949, Sarojini Naidu died at Lucknow, Uttar Pradesh.

BHOGARAJU PATTABHI SITARAMAYYA

(Born 24 Nov., 1880)

"Bhogaraju Pattabhi Sitaramaya, former President of the Congress and the Governor of Madhya Pradesh was famous for authoring the history of the Congress. He was a member of the Constituent Assembly from the State of Madras. He was member of the Committee of Adoption of the National Flag, Rules of Procedure Committee, Steering Committee."

Dr. Bhogaraju Pattabhi Sitaramayya was born in a Telugu Niyogi Brahmin family on November 24, 1880 in Gundugolanu village, Krishna district (now part of West Godavari district) in Andhra Pradesh, was an Indian independence activist and political leader in the State of Andhra Pradesh.

Pattabhi graduated from the prestigious Madras Christian College, fulfilled his ambition to become a medical practitioner by securing a M.B.C.M. degree. He started his practice as a doctor in the coastal town of Machilipatnam, the then headquarters of Krishna District and the political centre of Andhra. He left his lucrative practice to join the freedom fighting movement. During the years 1912-13, when there was a great controversy over the desirability of forming a separate province for Andhra, he wrote a number of articles in "The Hindu" and other journals explaining the need for immediate formation of linguistic provinces.

At the Lucknow session of the Congress in 1916, he demanded the formation of separate Congress circle for

Andhra. The demand was opposed by Mahatma Gandhi, but as Tilak supported Pattabhi, the Andhra Congress Committee came into existence in 1918. He was a member of the Working Committee of the Congress for a number of years and the President of Andhra Provincial Congress Committee during the years 1937-40.

He ran for the presidency of the Indian National Congress as the candidate closest to Mohandas Gandhi, against the more-radical Subhas Bose in Tripura Session of 1939. He lost owing to Bose's rising popularity and the belief that Pattabhi favoured the inclusion of Tamil-majority districts in a future Telugu state in independent India.

Serving on the Congress Working Committee when *Quit India* was launched in 1942, Pattabhi was arrested with the entire committee and incarcerated for three years without outside contact in the fort in Ahmednagar, Maharashtra. During this time he maintained a detailed diary of day-to-day life during imprisonment, which was published later as *Feathers and Stones*. He is also the author of *The History of the Congress* published in 1935 with an introductory note given by Rajendra Prasad. His other popular publication was *Gandhi and Gandhism.*

He ran successfully for Congress presidency in 1948, winning with the support of Jawaharlal Nehru, the Prime Minister of India. He was a member of the J.V.P. Committee (Jawaharlal Nehru, Vallabhbhai Patel and Pattabhi) which recommended the formation of Andhra State without Madras City. Prior to this he served as a member in the Constituent Assembly, in 1952 he was elected to Rajya Sabha. Pattabhi also served as the Governor of Madhya Pradesh from 1952 to 1957. He established Andhra Bank in Machilipatnam on 28 November, 1923 which is currently one of the major commercial banks of India. He also started Andhra Insurance Company and Bhagyalakshmi Bank.

SARDAR VALLABHBHAI PATEL

(31 Oct., 1875 – 15 Dec., 1950)

"Sardar Vallabhbhai Patel popularly known as the Iron man of India. He was the first Home Minister of free India and Deputy Prime Minister. He is the Architect of United India by ringing the states into the Union by amalgamating them with the adjoining provinces. He was the Chairman of the Constituent Drafting Committee and was the member of the Constituent Assembly from Bombay State. He was also the member of the Advisory Committee, Fundamental Rights, Minorities, Tribals & excluded areas and Steering Committee."

Sardar Vallabhbhai Patel has played a vital role in India's independence struggle. He was one of the pioneer lawyers who had played a very prominent role in India's fight for independence.

Sardar Vallabhbhai Patel belonged to the famous clan of *Lewa Patidars* who had played a notable part in the history of Gujarat. They were Gujjars who came from Punjab and had occupied the rich charotar lands between the Mahi and Tapti rivers. Sardar Patel was born at Nadiad on 31st October, 1875. He was the fourth boy in the family. Vallabhbhai's earlier education was in two stages. He had first to complete the course in Gujarati before he started his education in English. He passed his final examination at the age of 13. He had matriculated at the age of 22. Even at school, Sardar Patel showed promise of his skill in handling men of diverse nature. He knew how to command and also how to get the best out of his team. The legal profession appealed to Sardar Patel, as it would give him a feeling of independence. He passed his law examination in 3 years and became a District Pleader and started independent practice at Godhead in 1900. Within two years he acquired sufficient experience and confidence in legal practice. In 1902, he shifted to Borsad which offered him greater scope for these activities. Within 3 years, he had put up means to satisfy his longing to go to England and qualify as Barrister. In 1910 August, he left for England. He was greatly struck with the spirit of law that pervaded the entire legal structure and he found that the British People cherished their rights and would not permit any infringement of them. It appeared to him that as soon as Englishmen crossed the Suez Canal, their mentality changed into that of world conquerors, a superiority complex which relied on brute force to maintain its supremacy. In February, 1913 he was called to the Bar and returned to India. As a Barrister, his legal status had gone up. He had set up his practice at Ahmedabad. Sardar Patel had specialized in criminal law and rose to the front rank. He was fearless and bold and he did not mince words even if court's impartiality was to be impugned.

Gandhiji had returned to India from South Africa in 1915 with a big reputation and his unique achievements. Gandhiji had presided over the Gujarat Sabha and elected Sardar Patel as its Secretary thus bringing two dynamic personalities together. Two of them made a strong appeal and re-juvenated the Sabha. The Sabha came into an active conflict with the Government and in 1918 on account of failure of the crops the farmers of Kaira District had approached the Sabha. Sardar Patel took up their cause and wrote to the Commissioner. On February 16, Gandhiji agreed to lead people's struggle and Sardar Patel became his deputy. He discarded his Western dress and wore Dhoti and Short Coat. He walked from village-to-village, sat with peasants and shared their homely meals. The Barrister had become a peasant again. Gandhiji was enamoured of Sardar Patel's talents. Gandhiji said about Sardar Patel thus, "if it was not for his assistance, I must admit that the campaign would not have been carried through so successfully".

Vallabhbhai's exuberant nature carved a larger field of action than that of a successful criminal lawyer. He was essentially a man of action and wanted to do useful public work. He looked around, and Ahmedabad Municipality, which was in the doldrums, soon caught his eye. Vallabhbhai considered this a challenge and accepted it. He was elected to the Municipality in 1917. After fresh elections in 1924, Vallabhbhai was elected President of the Municipality and devoted all his time to its affairs.

To Vallabhbhai, this period was one of training in public life and administration. He had to manage men of diverse views and interests and in Gandhiji's words, "if we are unable to run our village (municipal) administration skilfully, honestly and justly, how can we justify our demand for the independence of our country?" Vallabhbhai injected a spirit of enthusiasm and zeal into the officers working under him.

Side-by-side with his municipal activities, Vallabhbhai was being drawn more and more into the political struggle. The magnetic force of Gandhiji drew him into it. The Rowlatt Bills were published in 1918 while Gandhiji was convalescing in his ashram. They shook his faith in the *bona fides* of Britain towards India.

In connection with civil disobedience movement started by Gandhiji there were disturbances in Gujarat. The aftermath of these disturbances in Gujarat was that the people of Ahmedabad had to pay a fine of nine lakhs of rupees, to be collected from all people except those exempted by the Collector. On account of his membership of the Satyagraha Sabha, the District Judge, Ahmedabad moved the High Court to declare Vallabhbhai and certain other lawyers unfit for practice in courts of law, until they had renounced their membership of *Satyagraha Sabha*. Sir Chimanlal Setalvad appeared in the High Court on their behalf and argued that the pledge of *Satyagraha* did not render the lawyers unfit for their profession, as no moral turpitude was involved. As a matter of fact, they had taken a pledge to behave in accordance with the principles of non-violence and to prevent any harm being done to anybody. The High Court did not accept this argument, but contended itself with giving them a warning. The great sacrifice made by Sardar Patel was that he had to give up his entire practice except for defending the persons prosecuted in connection with the disturbance and proving their innocence.

In 1920, Gandhiji was marching ahead with the plan of non-cooperation, and in a special session of Congress, non-cooperation was adopted as the creed of the Congress. Sardar Patel took pioneering part in the said movement.

It was in this atmosphere of confidence and buoyancy that the Congress met next year at Ahmedabad. Vallabhbhai was elected Chairman of the Reception Committee and he had to make the arrangements for holding the session and lodging the delegates. He detested pomp and pageantry and struck a note of simplicity and austerity. The movement was started with an enthusiasm and confidence but on February 8, 1922, violent disturbances flared up in Chauri-Chaura and Gandhiji suspended the civil disobedience campaign in Bardoli. Despite the action of Gandhiji and calling off the agitation, he was tried and sentenced to six years' imprisonment.

Sardar Patel became an ardent follower of Gandhiji and his life centered around him. He followed Gandhiji as a devoted disciple. It became his mission in life to fulfil Guru's idea and follow the path indicated by him.

In Gandhiji's absence Gujarat looked to Vallabhbhai for guidance, and he was popularly known as the *Suba* (Governor) of Gujarat. He set his heart on completely fulfilling Gandhiji's programme of constructive work among the people.

The tricolour flag with the *Charkha* in the centre had been solemnly adopted as the National Flag by the Congress in 1920. It represented the hopes and pledges of the people, but to the British it became a symbol of revolt.

Prohibitory orders were issued by the Government. However, the Congress Committee of Nagpur sent ten volunteers to defy it. The All-India Congress Committee requested Vallabhbhai to take charge of the *Satyagraha,* which had become a matter of prestige for the Congress. Sardar Patel took up the matter by his skilful manoeuvre and made the Governor to agree to the National Flag being carried and hoisted. Vallabhbhai had maintained the prestige of the Congress at a critical stage when the *Satyagraha* was at its lowest ebb. He vindicated the freedom of the flag when Borsad, his *taluka,* appealed to him for help. It suffered from the ravages of dacoits who appeared to be operating under a licence from the police.

On imposition of a punitive tax, Sardar Patel had advised people to resist payment of the tax provided they were prepared to undergo the necessary sacrifices and remain non-violent throughout the struggle. The Government, therefore, admitted its mistake and immediately remitted the tax. The people had triumphed in a short struggle of three months. When Gandhiji met him after his release from jail in February, 1924, he hailed Vallabhbhai as 'King of Borsad'. He was happy that his able lieutenant had once again proved the value of non-violent resistance and that he had developed discipline and unity among the people of Borsad. Vallabhbhai had shown once more that he was a consummate organizer.

A resolution was moved and passed by Pandit Motilal Nehru congratulating Sardar Patel at the Congress Session in Calcutta. He was tremendously applauded. Sardar Patel was pressed upon to accept the Presidentship at the behest of Gandhiji. He toured various States including Maharashtra, Karnataka and Bihar. In all his speeches he struck a note of rebellion against tyranny, and urged self-reliance and unity to fight it. A resolution demanding Dominion Status was approved by the Congress with a notice to the Government that direct action would be taken if the grant of Dominion status was not sanctioned before December 31, 1929.

While addressing a large gathering, Sardar Patel was arrested at Ras on March 7, 1929 and treated like common criminal. At the time of famous Dandi March on the issue of Salt Tax, Sardar Patel was in jail and on his release from jail on June 26, 1929 he took up the responsibilities of the President of the Congress. As President of the Congress, Sardar protested to the Government against the repression of the peasants in U.P. In reply the Government issued an Ordinance making it an offence to advise the tenants not to pay rent to the landlords.

The Congress, therefore, met at Lahore in December, 1929 in a mood of rebellion. It declined to participate in the Round Table Conference. It declared complete independence to be the goal of India and sanctioned the starting of civil disobedience on a country-wide basis.

All public meetings and processions were banned; the Congress offices and ashrams were raided and sealed. Lord Willingdon was doing everything possible to crush the Congress within six weeks as he had promised.

Sardar Patel remained in prison for 16 months with Gandhiji and the jail life brought the *Guru* and *Chela* together. Sardar Patel was trusted lieutenant of Gandhji and Gandhiji paid him rich compliments for his organizing spirit. During this time his brother Vithalbhai died and the Government agreed to release him for two days on conditions that he should not make political speeches. However, Sardar Patel declined to accept these conditions. On July 14, 1934, Sardar Patel was released from jail and he was a sick man at that time.

For the next Congress session at Haripura, Sardar's name was proposed for Presidentship by some Committees. But Jawaharlal Nehru was also a candidate. Sardar did not want to contest, so he advised the Congress to elect Nehru.

In 1937 elections were held to the Provincial Legislature. Sardar toured Maharashtra, Central Provinces, Gujarat and the South to organize the election campaign. The election results were a triumph for the Congress. Sardar Patel kept a tight grip over the work of all the Congress Ministries.

In 1939 the next session of the Congress was held at Tripuri and was marked by a clash between two Giants – Gandhiji and Subhash Chandra Bose. There were differences regarding election of the Congress President. Gandhiji and Jawaharlal Nehru appealed to Subhash Chandra Bose to withdraw his candidature in favour of Pattabhi Sitaramayya. There was show down at the Tripuri session. A resolution moved by Subhash Chandra Bose was rejected and the resolution of the Working Committee was passed, which had curbed the time honoured discretion of the President to nominate his Working Committee. Subhash Chandra Bose resigned as President of the Congress. Vallabhbhai persuaded Rajendra Prasad to accept the Presidentship.

On September 3, 1939, Britain declared war on Germany and the same day the Viceroy linked India as an ally of the British. The British claimed that they had to be fought for. Regarding British attitude of questioning the fitness of India for the grant of independence, Sardar Patel said, "you agree to give whatever a constituent assembly, composed of representatives of all the people, recommends. If you accept that, we shall do our best to come to an agreement with the Muslims".

The hand of co-operation extended by the Congress was summarily rejected by the Viceroy. The Congress Ministries in the Provinces were directed to resign by October 31, and they did so promptly. Communal rivalry had assumed deadly forms in its efforts to snatch favours and patronage from the Government. The communal outbreaks suited British policy. Now they were showing their hand by urging that India was not fit for self-government because of acute communal differences. In the meantime Muslim League led by Mr. Jinnah continued developing its two-nation theory until it found expression in a formal resolution of the Muslim League in 1940. The Muslim League dictated to the British and actually obtained an assurance from them that no constitutional changes would be made without the approval of the Muslims. The Muslim League had become a close ally of the British Government. Gandhiji, therefore, evolved the idea of launching individual civil disobedience as a moral protest against India's involvement in the war.

In December, 1941 the war took a grave turn. Mr. Winston Churchill, Prime Minister of U.K. had agreed to send Sir Stafford Cripps to find a solution to the Indian problem. Cripps came to India on March 23, 1942 with a proposal for an interim government leading to full self-government. Sardar Patel rejected the offer as it was designed to keep the British Authority firmly in India even after the war.

All-India Congress Committee was to meet on 27th April, 1942 and Sardar Patel attended the meeting in spite of his poor health. It debated the matter for 5 days before passing the famous "Quit India Resolution". It called upon the people to adopt complete non-cooperation towards the invading forces by withholding all assistance to them.

On August 8, 1942 the AICC passed the resolution asking the British to quit India. While supporting the resolution, Sardar recounted the efforts of the Congress to secure a peaceful transfer of power and said, "Do implement these suggestions. If all those who assist in the Government administration stand aside, the administration must necessarily break down.... Take up the message of the Congress and Mahatmaji and make the name of your country great". The Quit India resolution, adopted after midnight, was flashed throughout the world. In India it created a great sensation. Early next morning all leaders of the Congress were arrested.

Arrest of the Congress leaders led to country-wide protests. In Delhi, for example, the police opened fire 47 times in two days to frighten the crowds. About 60 persons were killed during the first few days. Over a lakh of persons were arrested, and according to official figures the casualities between 9th of August and the 30th of November, 1942 were 1,028 persons killed and 3,215 seriously injured. But the situation was brought under control.

Earlier in the morning the members of the Working Committee including Sardar Patel were taken away and lodged at Ahmednagar Fort. During the long-term detention, Sardar's health broke down frequently. Sardar Patel was released on 15th June, and thereafter he immediately met Mahatma Gandhi. Sardar Patel also attended the Simla Conference. The political events in England were taking decisive turn and the Labour Party which was sympathetic to Indian nationalism formed the

Government in July, 1945. A High Powered Cabinet Mission consisting of Lord Pethick Lawrence, Secretary of State for India, Sir Stafford Cripps and Mr. A.V. Alexander were also sent to meet leaders of all parties and try to reach an agreement acceptable to them. On May 16, it announced its own Plan for the future pattern of Government and invited the Parties to accept it. The Congress declared that the Plan was cumbersome and impractical and rejected it – except with regard to setting up a Constituent Assembly. On July 27, the Muslim League withdrew its acceptance of the Plan and declared that it would take direct action to achieve Pakistan. It nominated August 16, as the 'direct action' day. Jinnah said: 'Today we bid good-bye to constitutional methods.' The effect of the direct action was felt in Bengal wherein there was bloody carnage. At least 4,000 people were killed and thousands were wounded; property worth crores was destroyed by loot and arson. From there, the conflagration spread to Bihar on October 29, where a Hindu majority retaliated on the Muslims. This led to fast by Gandhiji in Noakhali.

The 'direct action' launched by the Muslim League followed by the blood-bath in Calcutta, had unnerved the British. The Viceroy, therefore, invited Pandit Nehru who had been elected President of the Congress, to form the Interim Government with the co-operation of the Muslim League – if he could get it. On August 24, he presented to the Viceroy a list of twelve members, selected by the Congress. They consisted of six Hindus – including one Harijan – three Muslims, one Christian, one Parsi and one Sikh. The Viceroy accepted the proposal and the Interim Government with Nehru as Vice-President of the Council was formed on September 2, 1946.

Strong and firm administration was necessary and Sardar performed a great national service by retaining the Home portfolio in his hands. In spite of the League's incitement, Sardar's foresight enabled him to handle the situation and to localize the disturbances in Punjab, Sind, Bengal and a few towns outside these provinces. Their leaders stated publicly that they had joined the Interim Government only to sabotage it from within. The communal flames lit in Calcutta, Noakhali and Bihar had been smouldering in the minds of men and now burst with violence in Punjab. With his uncanny foresight, Sardar came to the fateful decision that unless the country was partitioned, chaos and anarchy would spread throughout the land. The Congress Working Committee took a realistic view and agreed with him. The Indians were fortunate in having change of the Viceroy. Lord Mountbatten with a distinct record of leadership had taken over as the Viceroy of India on 22nd March, 1947. He ascertained that Jinnah was willing to accept Pakistan on the basis of division of Punjab and Bengal. Jinnah characterised it as 'moth-eaten Pakistan' but was content with it, because the Muslim League would thereby get control of the whole of N.W.F.P. and part of Punjab, which had been opposing it effectively. The new dominions would be set up on August 15, 1947. The AICC meeting held on June 14, 1947 also favoured the partition formally. However, Gandhiji was clearly against accepting the partition at any cost.

Widespread trouble broke out in West Punjab. Hindus and Sikhs fled from villages to the cities but could find no protection. They were looted, tortured and killed like helpless sheep under the knife of a butcher. The news of these atrocities flashed to East Punjab where the Hindus reacted with equal ferocity. It appeared as if the Hindus and Sikhs in West Punjab and Muslims in East Punjab had been trapped in hostile lands without any protection. These columns of refugees were often 10 to 12 miles long – the longest was 53 miles long -- in which men, women and children were fleeing from terror to the promised land of security. The bloodshed in Punjab flowed in all directions. Many of the refugees came to Delhi where they soon formed one-fourth of the population. They came in piteous condition, having lost their loved ones, their property and even their faith in the goodness of human nature. They brought with them gruesome tales of barbaric acts, looting and killing, bestial atrocities on women – capture and distributed as booty – and even spearing of children. Passions rose high and reached a pitch of mass-hysteria. The firm and timely action taken by Sardar gradually brought the turbulent elements under control[1].

The present day unified India owes its existence to Sardar Patel. Britishers had hoped that after their departure from India and transfer of sovereignty to the Princes of the States, the Princely State will declare independence and India will disintegrate. But for the Sardar's astute diplomacy this did not happen and in a short span of one year all the Princely States acceded the Union of India. The only two exceptions *viz.* Junagarh State & Hyderabad State were later made to acceded after an armed conflict. He was rightly called the ***iron man*** of India.

Sardar Patel firmly believed in having a strong judiciary which should be independent of the Executive. The Provincial Constitutions Committee of which Sardar Patel was the Chairman made the Judiciary independent of the control of the Executive and linked it effectively with the Supreme Court. As a Home Minister, Sardar Patel took active steps in overhauling the administrative machinery.

He kept the subversive forces in the country under check. He also maintained the effective control of the Centre over the State Governments. 1950, the last year of his life was marked by special vigour in all his activities.

---

1. K.L. Punjabi: The Indomitable Sardar, Published by Bharatiya Vidya Bhavan.

ASAF ALI

(May 11, 1888 - April 1, 1953)

"Asaf Ali was the member of the Constituent Assembly from Delhi who made valuable contribution in framing of the Constitution of India and member of the experts Committee."

[1]Asaf Ali was an India's independence fighter and noted Indian lawyer. He was the first Ambassador from India to the United States. He also worked as the Governor of Orissa.

Educated in St. Stephen's College, Delhi and called to Bar from Lincoln's Inn in England, he entered the Indian independence movement and was imprisoned many times. In 1928, he married Aruna Ganguli, a marriage that raised eyebrows on the grounds of religion (Asaf Ali was a Muslim while Aruna was a Hindu) and age difference (Aruna was 22 years junior to him). He was elected in 1935 as a member of the Central Legislative Assembly from Delhi representing the Muslim Nationalist Party. He was re-elected as a Congress candidate against a Muslim League candidate. He worked as Deputy Leader of the Congress Party in the Assembly.

---

1. The great Indians by One India One People Foundation in collaboration with Authorspress.

Asaf Ali was a patriot and humanist. Asaf Ali was one prominent public personality among the patriotic Indian Muslims who rejected the concept of nationhood based on religion. His was a many-sided personality-scholar, lawyer, nationalist, writer and connoisseur of music and arts – a remarkable product of the synthesis of Hindu and Islamic culture and of Indian and western values. Asaf Ali, born on May 11, 1888 in Delhi had his education in an Anglo-Arabic School and graduated from St. Stephen's College, Delhi. On graduation, Asaf Ali decided to qualify for the Bar and joined Lincon's Inn in England. In January 1912, he returned to India after doing his law. Not happy with the prevailing conditions on his return to India, he decided to go back to England and set up practice at the Privacy Council Bar. But again in 1914, he came back to India. Impelled by the nationalist fervour, stirred by Tilak and Annie Besant, he along with other like-minded people opened a branch of the Indian Home Rule League at Delhi. His witty and fearless denunciation of the government attracted large number of people to the Home Rule League. It was Asaf Ali who roused the political consciousness of the middle-class. Asaf Ali, who had created political consciousness with zeal, organized the annual session of the Indian National Congress in Delhi in 1918. The Delhi Congress was a demonstration of his organization skills. He was drawn into the Khilafat Movement which was essentially an expression of religious emotionalism. He played a noteworthy role in the boycott of foreign goods.

Asaf Ali always thrived on hard and sincere work. The arrival of the Simon Commission in 1928 provided another occasion for the exercise of his organizational talents. He took active part in the second Civil Disobedience Movement launched by Gandhiji in early 1930. Asaf Ali was arrested under the Defence of India Act and sentenced to one year's imprisonment. Later, he was elected to the

Central Assembly. He worked as his party's chief Whip, Secretary-General and Deputy Leader for twelve years.

He was among the first to volunteer for the Individual *Satyagraha* initiated by Gandhiji in 1940. He also stressed the need for Hindu-Muslim unity and non-violence. As a great patriot, he actively participated in the Quit India Movement of 1942. The All-India Congress Committee had passed a special resolution which called upon the British to Quit India. During the movement, like most other Congress leaders, Asaf Ali too was arrested by the British. He was sent to jail for four years.

In 1945, Ali came to be the convenor of the INA defence team established by the Congress for the defence of the officers of the INA charged with treason later in November 1945.

Asaf Ali defended Shaheed Bhagat Singh and Batukeshwar Dutt as a lawyer, after they threw a bomb in the Central Legislative Assembly on April 8, 1929, during the passage of a controversial ordinance.

When the Constituent Assembly was formed to draft the Constitution of India, Asaf Ali was a natural choice. As a member of this august assembly, he made valuable contribution to its work.

He was the Minister-in-charge of the Railways and Transport in the interim Government of India from September 2, 1946 before serving as the first Ambassador from India to the USA from February 1947 to mid-April, 1948. He was appointed the Governor of Orissa but he resigned from the post in May 1952 on health grounds. His last assignment was as India's Ambassador to Switzerland, Austria and the Vatican; he died in office in Berne.

In later life, Asaf Ali, an ardent nationalist, was appointed as Indian Ambassador to Switzerland in 1952.

Eleven months after taking charge of the assignment in Switzerland, Asaf Ali died of cardiac arrest at Berne on April 2, 1953.

SUBJECT INDEX

A

Adoption of Constitution
Dr. B.R. Ambedkar's speech—
November 25, *1949*, 100
November 26, *1949*, 10
Ambedkar's Speech Moving the Draft Constitution
Assembly-November 4, *1948*, 69

B

Biographies
Asaf Ali, 181
Benegal Narsing Rau, 143
Bhogaraju Pattabhi Sitaramayya, 167
Diwan Bahadur Alladi Krishnaswamy Iyer, 141
Dr. Babasaheb Ambedkar, 129
Dr. Rajendra Prasad, 117
Hansa Mehta, 155
K.M. Munshi, 147
N. Gopalaswami Ayyangar, 157
Pandit Jawaharlal Nehru, 121
Rajkumari Amrit Kaur, 159
Sachchidananda Sinha (1871-1950), 167
Sardar Vallabhbhai Patel, 169
Sarojini Naidu, 163
T.T. Krishnamachari, 151

C

Cabinet Mission, 1946, 21
Congress Resolution
Joint Parliamentary Committee Report, 14
Swaraj Constitution, 9
Constitution Making – First Attempt
Joint Parliamentary Committee Report, December, *1934*, 14
Nehru Report, August, *1928*, 10
Swaraj Constitution December, *1927*, 9

D

Dandi, 119
Draft Constitution as Revised by Drafting Committee
November 3rd, *1949*, 75

E

Election of Members of Constituent Assembly, 24
ex-Dewans of States, 25
ex-High Court Judges, 25
ex-members of Governor-General's Executive Council, 25
ex-ministers or Ex-Members of Governor's Executive Council, 25
ex-premiers of provinces, 25
ex-speakers of provinces, 25
ministers of provinces, 25
party leaders, 24
premiers of provinces, 25
speakers of provinces, 25
united provinces, 27

F

Final Adoption of Constitution
speech of Dr. Rajendra Prasad – November 26, *1949*, 108
Formation of Various Committees, 29
appointment of experts' Sub-Committees, 29
Fundamental Rights, 84
abolition of titles, 89
abolition of untouchability, 88
cultural and educational rights, 94

equality of employment opportunity, 88
final shape of articles, 98
prohibition of the discrimination, 87
protection against arrest and detention, 91
protection in respect of conviction for offences, 90
protection of life and personal liberty, 91
right against exploitation, 91
right to constitutional remedies, 96
right to equality, 86
right to freedom, 89
right to freedom of religion , 92
right to property, 95
sub-committee on minorities, 85

J

Jallianwala Bagh, 124

O

Objectives' Resolution
Nehru's speech on resolution, 52
Radhakrishnan's speech, 55
Opening Day of Constituent – Goodwill Messages
Dominions of British Commonwealth, 48
French National Assembly, 47
from Australia, 46
from the Republic of China, 46
from the United States, 45
Mahatma Gandhi, 49
Sachchidananda Sinha, 45, 46

Q

Questionnaire Issued by Constitutional Adviser
Amendment to Constitutions, 67
Executive, 60
Head of Indian Union, 57
Judiciary, 66
Legislature, 64
Quit India Movement, 15
August 8, *1942*, 15
August Revolution, 15
Bharat Choro, 15
Constituent Assembly, 15
Gowalia Tank, 16

R

Rules of Procedure and Standing Orders
adoption of National Flag, 82
credentials Committee, 80
finance and staff Committee, 79
house Committee, 80
order of business Committee, 82
steering Committee, 81
Sub-Committee, 81

S

Sabarmati Ashram, 119
Salt Satyagraha, 119
Simla Conference, July 1945, 20

W

Wavell Plan of 1945, 20
Working of Constituent Assembly, 35
Committees under the Constituent Assembly, 36
Indian National Congress, 36
list of members (by province/State), 40
members of the Indian Constituent Assembly, 36
Muslim League, 39

•••